# HR

# STRATEGIC
# PROJECT MANAGEMENT

# SPOMP

# Praises for "HR Strategic Project Management SPOMP":

"A refreshing and inspiring view on the project called change!"
— J. Harris, Chicago, IL

"The great thing about SPOMP is that it's independent of the methodology that you use. It complements PMBOK fully."
— V. Lloyd, Baltimore, MD

"Very readable, cohesive, clearly articulated, without the typical popular business management jargon."
— A. Salinger, Camden, NJ

"A must read for every modern internal HR project manager, program manager, or portfolio manager who wants to achieve change!"
— L. Wallowski, Philadelphia, PA

"I especially found the third SPOMP strategy very useful. Now I know how I can get the steering committee out of my chair."
— M. Codinio, Seattle, WA

"Top-notch insights about collaboration, engagement, and how to bridge the implementation gap."
— P. Vélez, New York, NY

"It's indeed not about the methodology, but about people and how to influence them."
— H. Tallis, Winchester, UK

"One of the most powerful books on Organizational Consulting that I've read in the past few years. Definitely a keeper!"
— W. Balog, Chicago, IL

"In a European project, Leon proved that a process plan based on communication moments lets you manage virtual teams very effectively."
— U. Gerstberger, Berlin, Germany

"One of the few books in this field that covers politics."
— Ch. Leibovitz, Staten Island, NY

"Proving the potential success of my project did it for me!"
— C. Jackson, Fort Worth, TX

"Logically structured, to-the-point, and a real pleasure to read!"
— TJ. Baxter, Wichita, KS

"An extremely agile approach to transformation, without losing control."
— A. Walker, Newcastle, Australia

"SPOMP increases your visibility in the organization enormously!"
— M. Ravdin, Montreal, Canada

# "Strategic Project Management SPOMP" is also Available for Internal Consultants from Other Departments, Including:

 **Financial** Strategic Project Management SPOMP (ISBN 978-0-9828779-2-0)

 **Marketing** Strategic Project Management SPOMP (ISBN 978-0-9828779-3-7)

 **IT** Strategic Project Management SPOMP (ISBN 978-0-9828779-4-4)

 **Legal** Strategic Project Management SPOMP (ISBN 978-0-9828779-5-1)

 **General** Strategic Project Management SPOMP (ISBN 978-0-9828779-6-8)

For more information, free excerpts, and links to retailers, please visit: www.SeduceStakeholders.com.

## Special Thanks to:

Accenture Plc
Apple Inc.
Bank of America Corp.
Campbell Soup Co.
Coca-Cola Co.
Comcast Corp.
Hartford Financial Services Group Inc.
Hewlett-Packard Co.
IBM Corp.
International Monetary Fund
Pepper Hamilton LLP
Sony Corp.
University of Chicago
University of Pennsylvania
World Bank

# HR

# STRATEGIC
# PROJECT MANAGEMENT

# SPOMP

Leon M. Hielkema

**Implementing Organizational Change Successfully:**
Five Powerful Strategies to Seduce and Influence
Stakeholders, Sell Your Ideas, and Boost Your Career
in the Human Resources Department

Copyright © 2012 by Leon M. Hielkema

First published in 2012 by LMHCpub.com

Content consultants: Ankie Swakhoven, BA/MBA and Mirjam Boelens, PhD
Chief editor: Darline Spring, PMP
Conceptual design: Annie Breeuwsma, Joii
Design illustrations and DTP: Fester Koekoek, Kuhasa DesignStudio

ISBN 978-0-9828779-0-6      Trade paper
ISBN 978-0-9828779-1-3      Ebook formats

Printed in the United States of America

10 9 8 7 6 5 4 3 2 1

# Dear Reader

Presumably, you are between the ages of 35 and 50 and well experienced in managing complex strategic projects. You work in the human resources department of a knowledge-intensive organization, with many highly educated professionals. The project teams that you lead comprise five to 10 members and the projects have an average duration of three to 12 months. Your projects stem from the organization's strategic mission, changing legislation, technological developments, efficiency measures, restructuring or, for instance, from the strategic agenda of the human resources department itself.

As an experienced internal consultant, project manager, program manager, management consultant, change agent, or change manager, your responsibility goes beyond that of an external consultant. You and your project team not only have to develop a solution, but also strategies and plans to implement this solution in daily practice.

"HR Strategic Project Management SPOMP" will give you new insights on how to successfully implement strategic change in your organization. It approaches change projects in a fundamentally different way. It does not focus on the project management technique, but on the process of influencing and persuading people. In other words, the focus is on "seducing" stakeholders into the change that you want to realize. In order to achieve this, concepts from the fields of psychology, project management, change management, and marketing are being utilized.

"HR Strategic Project Management SPOMP" is also innovatively structured. It is inspired by the Wikipedia search methodology, which means that you can decide the reading route through the content of this book. It does not matter if you start with reading the introduction, the index, or a subject in the table of contents that appeals most to you. All subjects are cleverly interconnected. Double brackets [] are used in the text to refer to paragraphs in this book, where the concerned subject will be explored in more depth. You will be able to get quicker (wiki is Hawaiian for "quick"), customized insights that fit your own change or project management style.

I firmly believe that the strategies in this book will bring you as much success as it has brought me and all internal consultants whom I have been coaching throughout the years. Please do not forget to post an online comment about this book. Your comment will help others in judging whether this book is suited to their specific situations. Thank you in advance and I wish you a lot of success with SPOMPing your future projects!

Chicago/Philadelphia,

Leon M. Hielkema, MBA

www.SeduceStakeholders.com
SPOMP@LeonHielkema.com

P.S. www.SeduceStakeholders.com/links contains updated links to leave your comments on Amazon, Barnes & Noble, Goodreads, iBooks, and many more. You will also find trusted links to my blog and social media venues like Facebook, Google+, LinkedIn, and Twitter. I am looking forward to hear from you!

# Contents

# Introduction

The ultimate goal of every strategic HR project is to effect change in your organization. This organizational change is successfully realized at the moment that "internal users" are utilizing the proposed solution in daily practice. Internal users are the stakeholders who have to change their behavior as a result of your project. They are the employees in your organization who have to change their daily routine, current way of working, or attitude.

The stakeholder in your organization who wants to accomplish this change is called the "client." The client is the individual who gives you the project assignment to develop an advice on how to implement change in your organization. Based on the advice you develop with your project team, the client will decide to execute the change strategies and plans that you recommend. Depending on your background, you may refer to the client as a project sponsor, line manager, CEO, principal, customer, project director, project owner, or executive sponsor.

Implementing change in your organization is a complex challenge. Research shows that only one third of all initiated projects are successful in meeting this challenge (Appendix A). Among the success factors, the formal project management technique (for example PMBOK, PRINCE2, MSP, Agile, etc.) that is applied only accounts for six percent of the project's success. The two most important success factors, however, are support from the client and support from the internal users, which together account for 34 percent of the project's success.

But how can you successfully create this support?

This book contains five strategies that are very powerful in creating support and buy-in for your change project or initiative. Combined, the strategies will create support by *seducing* (as in alluring or enticing) stakeholders into the change that you want to realize. *Seducing* stakeholders means that you influence them to become positive about the change. Creating this positive attitude will significantly increase your chances of a successful project.

## How to *Seduce* Friends

In my workshops, I always start with the example of *seducing* a group of friends to go skiing in January. Some friends will support your vacation plans, while others would rather go on a summer vacation. Some friends have children and prefer to go during a school break. Some friends prefer to go later in the year because January is a busy month at work for them, and some friends do not want to go on vacation at all. The key question is: How to *seduce* these friends to support your vacation plans?

Every group of friends has informal leaders. Probably, you will first try to *seduce* these informal leaders. If they are convinced, others will follow. You will also try to *seduce* those friends who are able to influence the informal leaders of the group. You will try to *seduce* them by communicating frequently about how fantastic a skiing trip would be, or how it has been a long time since you all went skiing together.

Furthermore, by letting your friends know that six mutual friends have already signed up for the trip, you are demonstrating the potential success of your vacation plans. You can make your plans sound even more favorable by communicating that you have found the perfect spot for the perfect price, but that this option expires within five days.

## How to *Seduce* Stakeholders

*Seducing* stakeholders works in a similar way as *seducing* friends to go on a skiing trip. You need to understand the politics in your organization to be able to determine which stakeholders need to be *seduced*. You need to frequently communicate with these stakeholders in order to continuously influence their perception about the change that you want to realize. You will have to convince stakeholders that change is inevitable and that your advice is the best option to implement this change. It is important to sell your project in order to tempt stakeholders to favor the change you are recommending. Also, to back up your arguments, you will have to prove during the project that your approach potentially will be successful in realizing organizational change. In a nutshell, if you want to *seduce* stakeholders, then you need to SPOMP your project.

**SPOMP Your Project**

The letters SPOMP are an abbreviation of the five strategies that are presented in this book (Figure 1). These five strategies are very powerful in *seducing* the client, internal users, and other stakeholders. Each strategy is a building block to become even more successful in implementing the organizational or behavioral change that you want to realize.

S  =  Select Your Stakeholders
P  =  Plan to Communicate
O  =  Organize Influence
M  =  Market Your Change Initiative
P  =  Prove Potential Success

**Figure 1**  Five SPOMP strategies to *seduce* stakeholders into change

**Select Your Stakeholders (S)**

Office politics always plays a major role when you want to realize change in your organization. Politics is often viewed as a negative force on the project, but you can turn it into a positive. To use politics as a positive force, you need to carefully select the stakeholders who can influence others to favor your project. Chapter 2 describes how to determine which stakeholders you need to select in order to use office politics to your advantage.

## Plan to Communicate (P)

In order to *seduce* stakeholders into change, you need to communicate on a frequent basis with them. This is essential in order to create multiple opportunities for yourself to positively influence stakeholders in adopting and embracing your change initiative. Frequent communication from the start of the project ensures that stakeholders are not confronted with a change, but that they are "taken along" in the change project. In this way, stakeholders will get accustomed to the idea of change, and this will significantly reduce potential resistance. Chapter 3 describes in two clear steps how to efficiently plan frequent communication moments with stakeholders.

## Organize Influence (O)

A steering committee, project board, or another governance body can help you to create support and buy-in for the change you want to realize in your organization. Chapter 4 describes how you can utilize such a body to successfully create this support. You will learn how to strategically organize your influence in such a way that the governance body will start working for you.

## Market Your Change Initiative (M)

Just as a manufacturer uses marketing to *seduce* customers into purchasing a product, you can use marketing to *seduce* stakeholders into change. Therefore, you need to view your change initiative as a product you want to sell to stakeholders. Chapter 5 describes how to sell your initiative by marketing your project, the capabilities of your project team, and yourself as the orchestrator of the change.

**Prove Potential Success (P)**

The challenge of the fifth and last SPOMP strategy is to prove during the project that your project will be successful in the end. The goal is to create a positive attitude from stakeholders regarding the organizational change that you want to realize. If you can convince stakeholders of this potential success, then it becomes much easier to *seduce* them into change. Chapter 6 describes how to *seduce* stakeholders by proving the potential success of your project.

**The Promise of SPOMP**

The five SPOMP strategies are very powerful in *seducing* stakeholders into change because it shows you who (S), when (P), and how (O, M, and P) to *seduce*. By SPOMPing your project, you will make the stakeholder's mind receptive to your ideas, even before implementing them in your organization. This greatly enhances your chances of realizing a successful change.

In addition, SPOMPing a project has many other advantages (Chapter 7). An advantage for the client is a shorter project duration because there is less resistance at the time the change is going to be implemented. Furthermore, internal users will benefit from SPOMP because they are able to influence the change process. Moreover, project team members will experience much more motivation to actively participate in the project because SPOMP delegates responsibility to them.

For you, the advantage is that SPOMPing a project will boost your career as an internal consultant (Chapter 8). You will be perceived as a successful professional because you are realizing change faster and better than others in your organization. As a result of your successful image, you will be asked to manage ever more interesting and challenging projects.

At a certain moment in your career, you can even choose which projects you would like to manage. The mere fact that you accept a project assignment will be considered as a "quality mark" within your organization.

Your successful image ensures that colleagues are keen to participate in the projects that you are managing. It will also create trust amongst stakeholders which makes managing future projects increasingly easy. I know this from my own experience and from the internal professionals whom I have coached over the years. It works in the same way as a football coach who has a successful track record and thus a successful image. He[1] also has no need to explain why he opts for a certain line-up.

Discover for yourself how you can SPOMP your project and success-fully *seduce* stakeholders into the organizational change you want to realize. Find out in everyday practice what SPOMP can do for you and how it will boost your career!

---

[1] Wherever the masculine term is used in this book, the female term also applies.

# Select
# Your Stakeholders

*Program manager Francesca and her team are preparing a plan on how to implement a Management Development strategy in their organization. The goal of the project is to improve work performance by developing coaching and leadership skills of senior management. Francesca's team interviewed several senior managers (internal users) and received positive feedback on the project goals. Although the client is closely involved, Francesca has the impression that she is losing his interest in her project. Several other projects have been launched in the meantime, and Francesca's project is sliding down on the organization's priority list. As a consequence, internal users tend to lose their interest in the project, too. Francesca wants to know how she can commit stakeholders to continue actively supporting her project.*

S upport and buy-in from the client and internal users are an absolute necessity when you want to realize a successful organizational change. The first SPOMP strategy "Select Your Stakeholders" (Figure 2) helps you to create support from both by using the stakeholders around them. You will learn which stakeholders you need to *seduce* in order to let the politics in your organization work for you.

| S | = | Select Your Stakeholders |
|---|---|---|
| P | = | Plan to Communicate |
| O | = | Organize Influence |
| M | = | Market Your Change Initiative |
| P | = | Prove Potential Success |

**Figure 2** SPOMP strategy: Select Your Stakeholders

In order to take advantage of the influential relationships between stakeholders, you need to map the political environment [2.1]. This is the arena in which you have to realize the desired organizational change. A powerful approach to map this political arena is to identify more stakeholders [2.2]. By stretching yourself to identify more stakeholders than you normally do, you will better recognize the influential relationships between them.

However, due to time and budget constraints, you cannot *seduce* all stakeholders in the political arena. A practical selection technique is the Target Group Approach [2.3]. This approach helps you to select the most important stakeholders. This is the critical mass that you need to *seduce* in order to get office politics working for you. Selecting these stakeholders will make you much more successful in implementing the change that you want to realize.

This chapter concludes with some important psychological insights from the Argumentation Theory. These insights are very helpful in persuading the client, internal users, and other stakeholders to support your project and the change that you want to realize. Research from this theory shows that besides the intrinsic quality of your argument, the structure and timing are important when persuading stakeholders [2.4].

> Some project management techniques (for example PMBOK) consider project team members as stakeholders, while others (for example PRINCE2) do not. In this book, project team members are excluded as stakeholders.

## 2.1 More Stakeholders Increase Your Power

Unlike external consultants, you are familiar with the stakeholders in the political arena due to previous projects or as colleagues within your organization. Therefore, you recognize more or less who will benefit from the change and who will benefit from maintaining the current situation (actual situation). This insight offers you a strategic advantage over external consultants. However, this advantage is often not used to its full potential as internal consultants tend to focus too much on the client.

If you focus primarily on the client in the political arena, then your role is often marginalized to doing what the client asks you to do. You will become dependent on the client because he is able to exert more political power than you are. The client's political power often leads to a solution that principally satisfies the needs of the client himself. Implementing this biased solution is likely to cause resistance from other stakeholders and often results in a cumbersome change process. Many organizational and behavioral change projects are failing due to the fact that the client has too much power and is coercing other stakeholders into change (Appendix A).

To increase your power you need to invite more stakeholders into the political arena [2.2]. Although this may sound counterintuitive, inviting more stakeholders will water down the power of the strongest political force. The reason that you now become less dependent on the political power of the client is that you created the opportunity to form coalitions [4.0] with the stakeholders that you invited. This will increase your political power because, theoretically, you only have to take sides to influence the decision-making process.

Inviting more stakeholders into the political arena will make you also more successful in *seducing* the client. This is because the client will be more easily *seduced* by another stakeholder in the political arena than by you as an internal consultant. This is especially true if you have a direct or indirect hierarchical relationship with that client.

The client's decision-making process to buy into your project is first and foremost influenced by the attitude of the internal users. If the client suspects resistance from the internal users, he will be more hesitant to actively support the organizational change. Secondly, his decision-making process is influenced by the attitude of other stakeholders. For example, if you get the client's boss to favor your project, then your project is likely to have the undivided attention of the client.

Suppose you have developed a new training program to complement the Management Development strategy. The client is satisfied and asks you to implement the new program in the organization.

During implementation, division managers appear to believe that too many courses have been included in the new program. They find the diverse training opportunities difficult to highlight in the annual job performance review with line managers.

In addition, the finance manager appears to believe that too many different training providers are involved. He pleads for a limited number of providers because this facilitates financial handling.

These negative voices will also reach your client. It is conceivable that these negative voices will undermine the client's commitment to your project.

The reverse may also occur. You have developed a new training program, but the client hesitates to implement the program in the organization. The client believes that the new program constitutes too much "fuzz" in the organization and will burden the resources of the HR department.

In this case, you would have been much more successful if you had invited more stakeholders into the political arena. Then, before advising the new training program to the client, you would already have consulted with the finance manager and division managers.

Suppose the finance manager considers the new training program a convenient opportunity to re-engineer the accounting process. The current process is very time consuming and has been an eyesore for years.

Suppose division managers become enthusiastic about your project because the new training program offers them much more opportunities to retain talented employees. The client who cancelled your project (or threatens to put on hold) will be influenced by these positive voices. For instance, division managers will ask the client why he cancelled this excellent project.

The client's initial resistance is reversed through the influence of other stakeholders. In short, by identifying more stakeholders, you become less dependent on the client's political power. Politics now will start working for you.

## 2.2 How to Identify More Stakeholders

To determine which stakeholders you need in order to let politics work for you [2.3], you first need to brainstorm with your project team about who is influencing whom in the political arena. A powerful approach to explore these influential relationships is stretching yourself to identify more stakeholders than you are used to doing.

In order to identify more stakeholders, your view on stakeholders should be changed. Traditionally, a stakeholder is defined as a party or person who has a stake or direct interest in the outcome of the project. However, this passive approach will fail to be sufficient if you want to use politics to reach your goal. Therefore, you need to inspire your project team to view a stakeholder as an instrument that can be used in the change process. A stakeholder should only be defined as a stakeholder if you think that you can use him to realize a successful change. Thus, defining a party or a person as a stakeholder should be a strategic choice made by you and your project team. This active approach to stakeholders will uncover unthought-of stakeholders and ensures that you invest your energy in identifying and analyzing the right stakeholders.

To identify all potential stakeholders in the political arena, you must distance yourself from the project. Look at how your project could contribute to the organization's strategic mission and which stakeholders would benefit from this. Identify also which stakeholders would be impacted by your project in the short term.

By distancing yourself, you could find that your own department is a potential stakeholder, as your colleagues can indirectly influence the client. Another stakeholder may be the finance department because their endorsement can positively influence other stakeholders. Try to identify all potential stakeholders in the political arena that can help you to use politics to your advantage.

Brown (2007) uses eight guidelines to identify potential stakeholders:[2]

- Follow the money. Whoever is paying for your project or is saving money as a consequence of your project is definitely a stakeholder.
- Follow the resources. Every entity that provides resources, whether internal or external, labor or facilities, and equipment, is a stakeholder. Line managers and functional managers providing resources are stakeholders.
- Follow the deliverables. Whoever is the recipient of the project result is a stakeholder.
- Follow the signatures. The individual who signs off on completion of the final product or service (or phases thereof) is a stakeholder.
- Examine stakeholder lists of other projects. Include active and completed projects.
- Review the organizational chart to asses which parts of the organization may be stakeholders.
- Ask team members, customers, and any other confirmed stakeholders to help you identify additional stakeholders.
- Look for unofficial influences. These may be people who are trusted by high-level leaders or who wield a lot of power through influence and not position.

Identifying more stakeholders helps you to map all actors in the political arena in which you have to realize your change. The next step is to find the influential relationships between these stakeholders (Figure 3).

---

[2] Brown, J.T., The handbook of program management, McGraw-Hill, New York, 2007, p. 54-55.

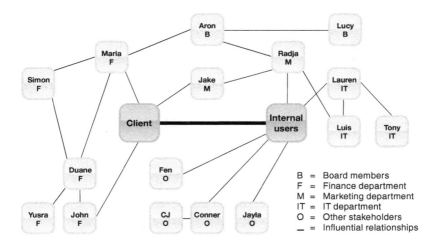

**Figure 3** Influential relationships between stakeholders

Once you have identified all potential stakeholders and their influential relationships, it is recommendable to record this stakeholder analysis in a document, the so-called stakeholder longlist.

By periodically reviewing this document with your project team, you will be able to monitor whether the influential relationships have changed in the political arena, whether new stakeholders have joined, or whether the relative power balance between stakeholders has changed. In other words, the stakeholder longlist helps you to periodically evaluate if you are using office politics to its full potential.

## 2.3 Target Group Approach

The stakeholder longlist [2.2] that you have created with your project team maps the complete political arena in which you have to realize your change. Once you have this "big picture" of all potential stakeholders, you need to select which stakeholders you actually need to *seduce* in order to let politics work for you.

A powerful technique to help you make this selection is the Target Group Approach. This approach consists of two steps. In the first step, you categorize all potential stakeholders from the stakeholder longlist into clusters of stakeholders (target groups). The second step is to determine per target group the most important stakeholders. The advantage of this Target Group Approach is that you keep the relative power balance in the political arena intact. This will make you much more successful in selecting the right stakeholders to *seduce*.

Imagine that you have to select players for the world's best soccer team. You decided to make a longlist of potential players from all over the world and to give points per individual player. The eleven players with the most points you intend to select for your soccer team. This approach will probably result in a team of many strikers, as strikers have the highest perceived value. In other words, selecting the best individual qualities does not always guarantee a well-balanced soccer team.

In order to create a well-balanced soccer team you should, before selecting individual players, first look at which positions in the team (field positions) need to be filled. You will need forward players, players for the defense and center, a keeper, and a striker.

Dividing the potential players into these target groups helps you to set an order of precedence and to select which player you need per position. This Target Group Approach makes you much more effective in selecting the right players whom you need for a successful soccer team.

Stakeholders from the stakeholder longlist should be divided into five target groups (Figure 4).

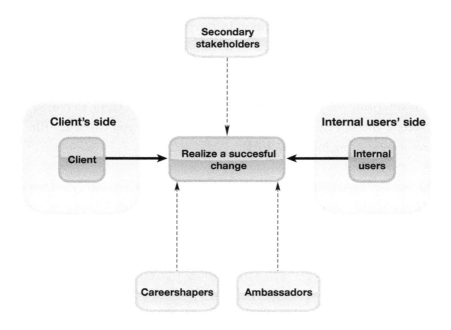

**Figure 4** Five target groups in the political arena

The first target group to select from the stakeholder longlist is called the "client's side" [2.3.1]. This target group includes stakeholders who are able to influence your client.

The second target group includes the stakeholders who have to change their behavior as a result of your project. This target group is called the "internal users' side" [2.3.2].

The third target group is the "secondary stakeholders" [2.3.3]. These are the stakeholders on the stakeholder longlist who do not belong to the client's or internal users' side, but who can influence your project and the change that you want to realize. Think in this respect for example of a Works Council.

You can strengthen your position in the political arena even further by paying attention to two additional target groups in the stakeholder longlist. These target groups are called "ambassadors" [2.3.4] and "careershapers" [2.3.5]. Ambassadors are the stakeholders who can help you promote your project and the change you want to realize. Careershapers are the stakeholders who can help you to secure the necessary staffing for your project.

The remaining stakeholders on the stakeholder longlist who could not be divided into one of these five target groups are apparently not playing a significant role in the political arena. In other words, you and your project team have decided that these stakeholders are not necessary to *seduce* in order to successfully realize the desired change.

## 2.3.1 The Client's Side

To determine which stakeholders belong to the client's side, you need to analyze the stakeholder longlist [2.2] on who is influencing your client. These so-called "indirect clients" can be the boss of your client and the bosses in the hierarchical line above that. They can influence the decision-making process of your client which makes them important candidates to *seduce*.

An indirect client can also be a problem owner. For example, a department manager experiences a problem and asks your boss to find a solution. Your boss gives this project assignment to you, so he is your client. As an internal consultant, you will have to decide if it is necessary to *seduce* this problem owner in order to realize a successful change. This decision depends on the power of your client. If your client has enough formal or informal power over the problem owner, then you can leave this responsibility to the client.

Depending on the project, other indirect clients can be a sponsor, members of the steering committee or project board, line managers, board members, or even a CEO. You need to analyze for each project assignment which indirect clients can influence your client. Analyzing the client's side enables you to carefully select which indirect clients you need to *seduce* in addition to the client. This will make you much more successful in realizing change.

> Executive support is generally considered as one of the most important success factors when realizing change (Appendix A). But who are these executives? Analyzing the client's side helps you to select the most important executives from whom you want support.

## 2.3.2 The Internal Users' Side

The internal users are the stakeholders who have to change their behavior (attitude or working method) as a result of your project. In the stakeholder longlist [2.2], you will probably find multiple stakeholders who have to change as a consequence of your project because a change generally impacts various areas in the organization.

Analyzing the internal users' side enables you to set an order of precedence. The internal user who undergoes the biggest or most radical change is the most important internal user to *seduce*. Depending on the project and the situation, you have to select which internal users you need to *seduce* in order to let politics work for you.

### 2.3.3 Secondary Stakeholders

Besides stakeholders on the client's or internal users' side, you also have to select secondary stakeholders from the stakeholder longlist [2.2]. Secondary stakeholders need to be *seduced* as a third target group because they also can influence the success of your project.

An example of a secondary stakeholder is a Works Council, as they have to approve or positively advise about the change you want to realize.

A Works Council is a democratically chosen committee of employee representatives within an organization, positioned between the management of the organization and the labor or trade unions. The goal is to involve employees in management decisions and to foster an atmosphere of trust and participation. For example in Germany, management cannot strategically change the organization without approval (or consultation) by the Works Council.

Other systems of joint decision-making can be found in countries like: Japan (Advisory Board), UK and Australia (Joint Consultative Committees), France (Comité d'Entreprise), Spain (Comité de empresa) and Sweden (Joint Project Groups). An organization with operations in at least two European Union member states is obliged to install a European Works Council.

In the U.S., employees have virtually no institutionalized role in management decision-making. The foundation of U.S. labor laws directly prohibits these forms of employee participation (National Labor Relations Act of 1935). As a result, U.S. management has more leeway in implementing organizational change, but on the other hand it also has to deal with large trade or labor unions on issues as wages, working hours, and safety.

Your department (or a project team member's department) can also be a secondary stakeholder. A project is very time consuming, time that project team members could otherwise spend on their own department's daily activities. Therefore, you have to *seduce* the department's colleagues by keeping them informed about the project developments [3.0]. By doing this, you foster understanding that the current priority temporarily lies with your project.

Other departments within the organization can also be a secondary stakeholder. For example, the quality management department has to adjust its policies as a result of your project. Another example is the communications department that needs to create an instruction manual for internal users.

Also think of the IT department, facilities services, and so forth. Ensure that these secondary stakeholders are being kept in the loop of the developments during the project [3.0], and do not confront them with the change at the moment of implementation. By keeping secondary stakeholders apprised, you will always be one step ahead of possible resistance during or at the end of a project.

The above mentioned examples of secondary stakeholders are situated within your own organization. However, boundaries between the organization and its surroundings are fading. Stakeholders can also increasingly be found outside of your own organization.

Imagine the involvement of a union representative in the development of the HR strategy, or the involvement of an external governance institute in the development of an accountability system. You could also think of the umbrella to which your organization belongs, ministries, trade organizations, shareholders' associations, member or consumer associations, special interest groups, loan agencies such as banks and credit institutions, local, state, and federal authorities, licensing agencies, the media, business associates, and the like. These external secondary stakeholders can influence other stakeholders in the political arena, which is the reason that you should consider involving them in your change project [3.0].

## 2.3.4 Look for Ambassadors

For the fourth target group, you have to select ambassadors from the stakeholder longlist [2.2]. An ambassador is a stakeholder who intrinsically favors your project from the start because he values its importance for the organization as a whole. An ambassador has the same project goal as you, but he does not interfere with how you go about achieving this goal. He is usually neutral in favoring the client's side [2.3.1] or the internal users' side [2.3.2].

An ambassador will promote your project and the change you want to realize. As an internal consultant, you want to utilize this positive force in order to foster goodwill from other stakeholders in the political arena. Therefore, you need to actively appoint and promote this ambassadorship. This is important for the marketing of your project, your project team, and yourself (I-marketing) as the orchestrator of the change [5.0].

Selecting ambassadors is not only important because they communicate favorably, but they also can provide valuable feedback and intelligence to the project team.

Suppose that you have selected an ambassador within the legal department who is willing to endorse your project. The information about the project that you provide this person with will be discussed within his department (for example during their regular weekly meeting). Thus, the legal department is indirectly kept informed about your project. Should resistance to the change arise from this department, then this valuable feedback will be passed on by this legal person to the project team.

Finally, you can use ambassadors to form strategic coalitions [4.0]. An ambassador is therefore an important stakeholder to select if you want to let politics work for you.

> The conscious use of ambassadors is also known as the "communication leverage effect." By involving a person from a certain group, this group will be informed via that person.
>
> A classical example is that of a top salesman, who for many years sold three times more life insurances than other salesmen in his company. Most of the other salesmen went door to door to sell life insurances. The top salesman, however, went to the chairman or treasurer of a neighborhood association. If he could persuade the chairman or treasurer, then this person became an ambassador for his product. Other members of the neighborhood association now were much easier to *seduce* because someone from their midst had already purchased a life insurance policy from this top salesman.

## 2.3.5  Do Not Forget Careershapers

For the last target group, you have to select the careershapers from the stakeholder longlist [2.2]. Careershapers are the stakeholders with whom you (or one of the project team members) have an authority relationship. Examples are a direct boss and the individuals in the hierarchical line above that.

Careershapers are important to select because they determine how much time project team members can allocate to the project. For example, by appointing the boss of a project team member as a careershaper, you ensure his involvement in the project. This involvement shields your project team member from other daily work and gives him the necessary latitude to actively participate in your project.

Selecting careershapers is also important because they can affect your own career. By involving them in your project [3.0], you can show your added value and better promote yourself (I-marketing) as a successful professional in your organization [5.4]. Make sure that you keep careershapers apprised of the project developments. This way, they know what you are doing, which will make it easier to endorse a future promotion request [8.0].

Stakeholders who can affect the career of each individual project team member should also be identified as careershapers. This will facilitate the marketing of your project team [5.3]. In case a project team member is employed by another department or unit within your organization, make sure that you keep his boss informed about the project's progress and the team member's contribution to it.

*Seducing* these careershapers will make you much more successful in getting the politics in your organization to work for you. As a consequence, you will become more successful in implementing the change you want to realize.

Every individual on the stakeholder longlist is connected to other individuals on this longlist. Individuals might know each other because they attend the same meetings or because they are part of the same team. The relationship between these individuals could also be outside your organization. For example, they might meet privately at a sports club.

Looking at these types of relationships could uncover that an important careershaper participates in a meeting in which one of your secondary stakeholders is chairman. In this case, it could be worth it to spend additional "seduction energy" on this secondary stakeholder because if you can persuade this secondary stakeholder to support your project, there is a good chance that your careershaper will be influenced positively as well.

## 2.4 Persuasive Communication

The Target Group Approach [2.3] is very powerful in selecting which stakeholders you minimally need to *seduce* in order to use office politics to your advantage. Once you have selected these stakeholders, you need to persuade them to support and buy into the organizational change you want to realize. But how important actually is the intrinsic quality of your arguments when persuading stakeholders?

At Harvard University, an interesting study was conducted regarding the quality of the argument when persuading people.[3] People queuing in front of a copy machine were observed to determine with which arguments those waiting were willing to let a student pass in front of them. To the question: "Could I use the copy machine because otherwise I will be late for class?," 94 percent of those waiting allowed the student to go first. To the question: "Could I use the copy machine?" (without giving a specific argument), still 60 percent of those waiting let the student go first. The results of the third group were even more surprising. Their argument was simply that "they had to make copies."

---

[3] Langer, E.J., Blank, A., and Chanowitz, B., The mindlessness of ostensibly thoughtful action: the role of "placebic" information in interpersonal interaction, Journal of Personality and Social Psychology, 1978, Vol. 36, p. 635-642.

This was a nonsense argument since everyone stood in line to make copies. Yet, 93 percent of those waiting let the student go first.

From this study, it appears that the quality of the argument does not matter if you want to persuade people. This study has been repeated many times, always with similar results.

Further research showed that the quality of the argument becomes increasingly important when the people waiting in front of the copy machine are more involved. If, for example, the copy paper is in short supply or the toner is low, then only 24 percent were willing to let the student go first without further reason. If the students gave a strong argument (for example "otherwise I will be late for class") then this percentage doubled. When giving a poor argument (for example "because I have to make copies") this percentage lowered again to 24 percent.

Based on this study, one can conclude that it is easier to persuade stakeholders when you give them an argument, and that the quality of the argument becomes more important when their involvement increases.

With a low involvement, it is better to use many arguments as to why your project is so important.[4] With a high involvement of the stake-holders, it is better to limit your arguments to three. It does not matter whether you start or finish with the strongest argument. Generally, though, the first and the last argument are often best remembered by the recipient.

---

[4] Petty, R.E. and Cacioppo, J.T., Communication and persuasion: central and peripheral routes to attitude change, Springer-Verlag, New York, 1986, p. 82-97.

The client's involvement is always high from the beginning of the project. According to the above mentioned study, you will need strong arguments in order to be able to persuade him. Internal users and other stakeholders often do not feel involved from the beginning of the project. So in order to get them involved in the project, you need to start communicating with them. The content that you communicate (or quality of your argument) is less important according to this study. A productive strategy to persuade or *seduce* these uninvolved stakeholders is to communicate frequently and give them as many arguments as possible [3.0].

As an internal consultant, you therefore need to investigate what every stakeholder considers a quality argument to change (i.e. "What's in it for him"). Subsequently, you have to balance these arguments for every project phase. Keep this in mind when you are planning communication moments [3.0] in your project. By repeating your arguments, you anchor the change that you recommend in the stakeholder's mindset. This way he gets accustomed to the change and is susceptible to being *seduced*. The power of a communication message lies in its repetition.

A powerful way to increase the quality of your change-argument is the SEXI model: State, EXplain, and Illustrate. First, briefly state your argument, then explain what exactly you mean by it (reasons why it is as such) and finally, illustrate it with an example or a source.

These three components make your argument more persuasive and ensure that your change message will resonate with the stakeholders. Applying this model also forces you to actually substantiate your argument. The SEXI model can be used for oral presentations as well as written reports.

Example of an argument constructed with the SEXI model:

Artists should be tested for drugs (State). As art lovers, we expect creative excellence from painters, directors, advertisers, authors, sculptors, and all others alike. In order to reach even higher creative performance, artists increasingly resort to alcohol and other mind-enhancing drugs (EXplain).

We do not permit top athletes either to use muscle-enhancing drugs to improve their performance. Therefore, we also have to protect artists against themselves by testing them for drugs (Illustrate).

# Plan to Communicate

*Tom and his project team are responsible for implementing a Talent Management strategy in their organization. They have analyzed the political arena and decided which stakeholders they need to seduce in order to realize a successful organizational change. Tom's team is designing a project plan to efficiently develop a solution. However, they are aware that just a solution will not be enough to seduce stakeholders into change. Stakeholders need to be involved during the development of the solution so as to prevent resistance at the moment of implementation. Tom foresees resistance from internal users, because they are the ones who have to make it work while they are least rewarded for the energy they have to put in. Tom is planning to conduct interviews and to organize workshops in order to involve internal users, but he wonders whether this will be sufficient to prevent resistance. To put it in Tom's words: "We plan to consult them, but do we reach their heart and soul?" Tom wants to know how he can seduce internal users in order to create support and buy-in for the change that he wants to realize.*

T raditional project management techniques (for example PMBOK, PRINCE2, or MSP) are very effective in producing an end product or service, such as an advisory report on how to implement organizational change. However, an organizational change cannot be realized with just a report. Realizing change is a process of communicating and interacting with multiple stakeholders. Therefore, your focus should not be on efficiently developing the report, but on the people that you want to *seduce*.

In order to *seduce* stakeholders into change, you have to start communicating and interacting with them before the change is going to be implemented. The second SPOMP strategy "Plan to Communicate" (Figure 5) helps you to design this process by organizing frequent communication moments in your project.

| | | |
|---|---|---|
| S | = | Select Your Stakeholders |
| **P** | **=** | **Plan to Communicate** |
| O | = | Organize Influence |
| M | = | Market Your Change Initiative |
| P | = | Prove Potential Success |

**Figure 5** SPOMP strategy: Plan to Communicate

Organizing communication moments in your project will keep the focus on the stakeholders whom you want to *seduce*. Every communication moment ensures that stakeholders are not confronted with a change (push-strategy) but that they get the chance to get accustomed to the change. This will significantly reduce potential resistance. In addition, every communication moment gives you the opportunity to pro-actively influence stakeholders and to gradually *seduce* them to buy into the change you want to realize (pull-strategy) [3.1].

To efficiently manage this process of frequent communication with multiple stakeholders, you need to plan [3.2] and organize [3.3] your project differently.

A powerful approach is to develop a process plan that is based on communication moments. This plan describes what, when, and how you are going to communicate with stakeholders. The advantage of creating such a plan is that you will *seduce* stakeholders to first commit to the process, before committing them to the end goal of your project. Committing stakeholders first to the "journey of change" makes it much easier to realize the end goal.

A traditional project plan is usually based on technical milestones such as an interview with an internal specialist that must be completed prior to a certain date. However, a process plan based on communication moments approaches a milestone from a different perspective. Inspire your project team to reformulate this technical milestone as: "Present the interview results on date x to stakeholder y." This puts the project team's focus on the communication and interaction with stakeholders, which will make you much more successful in realizing change.

A second advantage of a process plan based on communication moments is that you need significantly less effort to manage your project team [3.4]. As leader of the project team, you will evolve from a cop checking deadlines into a coach inspiring your project team members.

Finally, the process plan itself is a strong communication message to present to stakeholders at a communication moment. Presenting this plan will spark the interaction with stakeholders early in the project. This will not only create trust amongst stakeholders [3.5], but it will also increase your control on the project [3.6].

Your client gives you the assignment to implement Talent Management in your organization. Suppose you find an excellent report on the internet on this topic from an identical organization. What would happen if you deliver this advisory report to your client one hour after you have been given the assignment?

Your client will probably have many questions after reading the report. This is because it is not the report's content (i.e. knowledge transfer) but the interaction with the client that creates the support. The interaction prior to the advisory report gives the client the chance to become accustomed to your ideas. You allow the client to mentally grow towards the advice you are going to provide.

The same applies to internal users and other stakeholders. Delivering the advisory report without prior interaction is considered as an internet report and will evoke resistance. In order to create support for your ideas and to prevent resistance, you therefore need to organize frequent communication moments (interaction) with stakeholders. Frequent communication makes the stakeholders' minds susceptible to accept the change you want to realize with your project.

## 3.1 Frequent Communication Moments

Organizing frequent communication moments in your project helps you to put your project in the spotlight and to socialize your ideas.

Compare it for example with a television commercial. One broadcast or communication moment will not be sufficient to *seduce* customers into purchasing the product that is being promoted. Frequently communicating or broadcasting the commercial will significantly increase the sales of this product. This is because frequently exposing customers to a communication message subconsciously influences their decision-making process [5.0]. The mere effect of hearing about the product already positively influences their perception. This is why the majority of customers tend to choose the most familiar brand in a supermarket over a lesser known product. For the same reason, your project will be more successful if you communicate more frequently with stakeholders than you are used to doing.

In medical research, it is commonly known that the mere attention for a patient alone, like giving an inert pill, can already improve his medical condition.

This phenomenon is called the placebo effect. The patient believes that his illness is being treated, and this positively influences his perception about the treatment. By communicating more frequently, you give attention to stakeholders and this evokes a positive attitude towards the change that you want to realize.

The advantage of frequent communication moments is that you create the opportunity to gradually take stakeholders along in the change process. Every consecutive communication moment accustoms stakeholders to the idea of change, which will significantly reduce potential resistance.

Frequent communication moments will also trigger feedback from stakeholders with whom you are communicating. This frequent feedback during the project enables you to dynamically align your project to the ever changing reality. In addition, feedback from for instance internal users also provides you with arguments that you can use when you need to manage the client's expectations.

The most important advantage is that every communication moment offers an excellent opportunity to positively influence stakeholders. Positively influencing stakeholders, for example by selling your change initiative [5.0], is crucial when you want to *seduce* stakeholders into change. Therefore, you and your project team will have to design a process plan which facilitates frequent communication with multiple stakeholders [3.2].

## 3.2 How to Plan Your Communication Moments

Communicating more frequently per stakeholder and with more stake-holders than you are used to [2.0] will definitely make you more successful in realizing organizational change. But how can you plan and organize this process efficiently without increasing the total project duration?

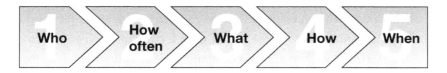

**Figure 6** Five steps to design the skeleton of your process plan

A powerful approach is to develop a process plan that is based on com-munication moments. In order to achieve this, you and your project team first need to design the skeleton of the process plan. You can efficiently design this skeleton by guiding your project team through the following five steps (Figure 6).

**Step 1: Who**
In this first step you should double check if you have identified all important stakeholders in the political arena [2.3]. Write these stakeholders for example on a flip-over, and list behind each

stakeholder their regular meeting schedule. This regular meeting schedule per stakeholder helps you to strategically plan the communication moments (See step 5) in your project.

## Step 2: How often

Secondly, you need to estimate with your project team how often a communication moment is needed per stakeholder. You will have to find a balance between the number of communication moments that you deem necessary to successfully *seduce* stakeholders and an efficient execution of the project. With each project, you have to determine how to balance between efficiency and effectiveness.

Determining how often a communication moment is needed per stakeholder is an educated guess at best. The advantage of first assessing the communication frequency is that you get a global time frame when a communication moment needs to be planned in your project. With these global time frames in mind you need to determine with your project team: "What can we present to stakeholders?"

## Step 3: What

In order to determine what to present on a communication moment, you need to revert to your technical view on project management. Together with your project team, you have to investigate which intermediate tangible products (i.e. deliverables, work products) are potentially brought forth by your project.

These intermediate products are traditionally designed to meet the client's needs, but with some minor adjustments, you can also use them to spark communication with other stakeholders. You are going to produce these products anyway, so why not re-use them to *seduce* internal users and other stakeholders? For example, think about products as an analysis of the current situation, results of the interviews that you have conducted, or a traditional progress report.

In addition to re-using the products that you create for the client, you can also consider creating a new product. This product, however, is not designed to serve the client, nor is it technically necessary to implement change. Instead, you will specifically design this new product to *seduce* a particular stakeholder. An example is an employee satisfaction survey that you deem necessary during your project.

The goal of this third step is to identify products that you can present on a communication moment to a stakeholder. These products are the vehicles to spark communication. The challenge is to make effective use of these products. That is why you have to inspire your project team members to view these products as communication messages that you can use to positively influence and *seduce* stakeholders.

For now, it is sufficient to identify the subjects of the communication messages. Restrain yourself from thinking about how to produce these communication messages [3.3] because this may interfere with the process of identifying a communication message for each communication moment.

Creating a communication message that effectively *seduces* stakeholders into change is an intellectually challenging endeavor. This is the reason why the last two SPOMP strategies are devoted to marketing your change initiative [5.0] and proving the potential success of your project [6.0] on a communication moment.

**Step 4: How**

Once you have determined what to present, you have to decide with your project team which medium you want use to convey your communication message. Sometimes an email, newsletter, or an intranet page is sufficient. Another option would be to organize a special meeting with a particular stakeholder.

The medium that you are going to use is a strategic decision. You must try to find a balance between the number of stakeholders that you want to reach and the impact that you would like to have on a specific stakeholder.

**Step 5: When**

Finally, you have to determine with your project team on which exact date and at what time you want to plan a communication moment with a stakeholder. The aim is to pre-plan all communication moments for the entire project in the agendas of each stakeholder. Pre-planning all communication moments significantly increases your control on the project [3.6].

A communication moment is best aligned to the regular meeting schedule of each stakeholder (See step 1). You can ask a relevant stakeholder for a few minutes during his regular weekly meeting to present your process plan. Tuning in to a regular meeting has a psychological advantage. Participants tend to experience the regular meeting as familiar and, therefore, are often more receptive to think constructively along with the ideas that are being presented. If a regular meeting is not convenient or practical, you will have to find another way to convey your communication message (See step 4).

By guiding your project team members through the above mentioned steps, you quickly get a complete overview of whom to *seduce*, at what moments in the project, and which products (communication messages) you are going to present.

Table 1 presents the skeleton of a process plan based on communication moments for implementing a Talent Management strategy. The table shows that the communication message "interview results," which is initially designed for the client, is re-used to spark communication with board members and line managers. In other words, with one communication message you are serving three stakeholders. This will definitely change the way you and your project team will design the questionnaire because you need to present results that are interesting to all three stakeholders.

Table 1 shows that the "interview results" are presented on July 16th to the client during a regular meeting, on July 20th to board members also during a regular meeting (combined with the process plan), and on July 22nd to line managers for which you are planning to organize a special meeting.

In Table 1, you can also find that the Works Council's first communication moment is planned on June 26th. On this date, you are planning to present the process plan. You also decided with your project team that the Works Council needs a communication moment every three months (Step 2) in order to *seduce* this stakeholder successfully. So your next communication moment with the Works Council will be on or about September 26th. Together with your project team, you will have to decide which communication message (Step 3) you want to present on this communication moment.

**Table 1** Skeleton of a process plan based on communication moments

| | Step 1 | | Step 2 | Step 3 | Step 4 | Step 5 |
|---|---|---|---|---|---|---|
| | Stakeholder (target group [2.3]) | Regular meeting schedule | Communication frequency | Subject communication message | Medium | Communication moment |
| | Client (client's side) | 06/04, 06/11, 06/18, 06/25, 07/02, 07/09, 07/16, 07/23, 07/30, etc. | once every 2 weeks | stakeholder analysis<br>process plan<br>baseline measurement<br>interview results<br>etc. | presentation<br>presentation<br>email<br>presentation<br>etc. | 06/04<br>06/18<br>07/02<br>07/16<br>etc. |
| | Line managers (internal users' side) | 06/21, 06/28, 07/05, 07/12, 07/19, etc. | monthly | process plan<br>interview results<br>etc. | presentation<br>presentation<br>etc. | 06/21<br>07/22<br>etc. |
| | Talents (internal users' side) | no regular meetings | once every 2 months | process plan<br>etc. | presentation<br>etc. | 06/21<br>etc. |
| | Board members (careershapers) | 06/20, 07/20, 08/20, etc. | monthly | process plan + interview results<br>etc. | agenda item<br>etc. | 07/20<br>etc. |
| | Colleagues in HR department (secondary stakeholders) | 06/07, 06/14, 06/21, 06/28, 07/05, etc. | monthly | process plan<br>etc. | presentation<br>etc. | 06/20<br>etc. |
| | Works Council (secondary stakeholders) | 06/26, 07/26, 08/26, etc. | once every 3 months | process plan<br>TBD<br>etc. | presentation<br>TBD<br>etc. | 06/26<br>09/26<br>etc. |
| | IT department (secondary stakeholders) | 06/08, 06/15, 06/22, etc. | once every 3 months | | | |
| | Finance dept. (secondary stakeholders) | 06/08, 06/15, 06/22, etc. | once every 3 months | | | |
| | Other departments (secondary stakeholders) | 06/08, 06/15, 06/22, etc. | once every 3 months | | | |
| | All organization members (secondary stakeholders) | no regular meetings | 2 times during project duration | | | |
| | Trade unions | no regular meetings | no | | | |
| | Stakeholders outside your organization | no regular meetings | no | | | |
| | Etc. | | | | | |

Once you have determined all communication moments and messages per stakeholder, you have developed the skeleton of your process plan based on communication moments. This skeleton is the blueprint for your "seduction strategy" per stakeholder.

## 3.3 Organize Individual Tasks

Once you have designed the skeleton of your process plan [3.2], you need to determine which individual tasks have to be executed in order to be able to present a communication message on each communication moment.

Consider the communication message "interview results" that you plan to present on July 16th to the client and several days later to board members and line managers (Table 1). Together with your project team, you have to brainstorm which individual tasks need to be executed so that this communication message can be delivered on July 16th. From this deadline, you need to calculate backwards in time as to which individual tasks need to be completed in order to meet that deadline.

This back-to-front planning is essentially also what you tend to do, for example, when organizing a party for family and friends. First, you determine the party date. From this endpoint on you determine which tasks have to be executed and when they need to be executed.

The advantage of back-to-front planning is that you keep the focus on the people that you want to *seduce*. This focus will help you to make practical choices in the project and to avoid losing yourself in academic elaborations (analysis paralysis). It also minimizes the project duration and the use of resources because only those tasks that contribute to a newsworthy communication message are carried out.

The individual tasks that are necessary to present the interview results on July 16th form together a subproject within the total project (Figure 7). The goal of this particular subproject is to produce a communication message that *seduces* the client, board members, and line managers into change.

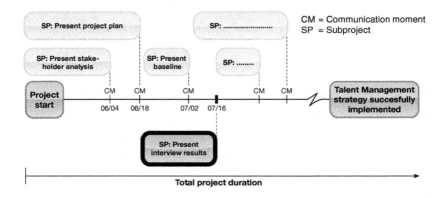

**Figure 7** Subproject "present interview results" on July 16th

You can efficiently manage this subproject by preparing an "action list" (also called a subproject schedule). This action list is a collection of individual tasks on which the project team members mutually agreed upon (Table 2). The result of an individual task has to be described as accurately as possible in the action list. Each project team member has to know exactly what is expected of him and when his task has to be completed.

**Table 2** Action list for the subproject "present interview results"

| Scheduled deadline | Individual tasks | Which project team member | Actually completed on |
|---|---|---|---|
| 06/19 | Inform the client that you need 15 minutes in the regular meeting of July 16th to present the interview results | John | 06/19 |
| 06/19 | Organize that the interview results will be discussed by board members during their regular meeting of July 20th | John | 06/19 |
| 06/19 | Schedule a meeting room and invite line managers for a meeting on July 22nd from 1 to 2 p.m. | John | 06/19 |
| 06/22 | Telephone interviews with two comparable organizations on how they implemented Talent Management | Carla | 06/22 |
| 06/25 | Research guidelines provided by law on performance incentives and email summary to the project team | Martin | no[5] |
| 06/29 | Interview Works Council President on how to map training needs per talent | Ian | 06/27 |
| 07/02 | Present draft questionnaire to project team | Lisa / Raul | 07/02 |
| 07/10 | Interview five line managers on implementing Talent Management | Raul | |
| 07/10 | Interview 20 talents | Lisa / Ian | |
| Etc. | | | |
| 07/14 | Practice presentation with project team | Ethan | |
| communication moment July 16th | Give presentation to client | Ethan | |
| communication moment July 20th | Give presentation to board members | Ethan | |
| communication moment July 22nd | Give presentation to line managers | Ethan | |

---

[5] My next book "HR Strategic Project Management PLUS" (expected 2013/14) describes what you can do if a project team member is not delivering on time. Other subjects covered in this upcoming book are presented on the last page of this book.

Of psychological importance is to leave the completed actions or tasks visible on the action list. This way, project team members can see the number of completed actions growing, which will motivate them to complete the remaining actions (that become less and less).

Also, leaving the completed actions on the list puts peer pressure on those team members that accomplish the least amount of work because their name will appear less frequently on the action list.

> "If you want them to build a boat, show them the sea." (part 1)
>
> Managing a project team does not necessarily mean that you have to impose actions on the project team members. Brainstorm with your project team about which actions are needed to develop a communication message and note these actions on a flip-over.
>
> As soon as all necessary actions have been identified, ask who wants to execute which action. It is important to first gather all actions and then attach a name to the execution of an action. This is because people often tend to stop contributing when their names are immediately linked to an action.
>
> In practice, project team members will volunteer because they find a specific action interesting, because the execution of the action fits within their daily planning, or because they want to avoid a less interesting action.
>
> Once a number of actions have been assigned, it automatically creates peer pressure on the less active project team members to sign up for the remaining actions.

By creating an action list per communication moment, you have created a very powerful tool to monitor and control your project. All action lists together are the mental contract that you and your project team members mutually agreed upon. In the following meeting(s) with the project team, you only have to follow up on the action lists in order to efficiently and effectively manage your project.

With an action list per communication moment, your total process plan based on communication moments is completed. The communication messages that are produced for each communication moment are designed to *seduce* stakeholders and to bring them along in the change you wish to achieve. This prevents potential resistance and will build commitment. A process plan based on communication moments helps you to intelligently divide your "seduction energy" among the stakeholders in the political arena [2.3]. It also provides a unique opportunity to reduce the energy that you need to manage your project team [3.4].

The results of the interviews should always be presented to the stakeholders who were interviewed. Stakeholders are in general very interested in these statistics. Furthermore, by presenting the results you evoke a response from these stakeholders. You can convey this response to other stakeholders on a communication moment. By doing so, you pro-actively create understanding for each other's opinions and the differences in interests. This will make it much easier to *seduce* stakeholders into change.

## 3.4 From Cop to Coach

You can significantly reduce your management efforts when you give a project team member full responsibility for a communication moment. This means that a project team member is managing the subproject [3.3] to produce a communication message and is presenting this communication message to stakeholders. By delegating the responsibility to give a real presentation, you make the project team member not only accountable to you as leader of the team, but also to the stakeholders to whom he is presenting.

This project team member will be very motivated to perform because he does not want to take a "nose dive" in front of the stakeholders to whom he will present. These stakeholders are direct colleagues, careershapers, or other stakeholders that you and your project team have consciously selected in the political arena [2.3].

Exposure to these stakeholders will stimulate this project team member to manage the subproject to the best of his abilities. He (and not you as leader of the team) will therefore encourage fellow team members to deliver quality and to meet the deadlines of the subproject. This project team member will consult with you on how to best present the results to stakeholders. As manager of the total project, you will transform from a cop who is monitoring deadlines into a coach who is inspiring project team members.

> "If you want them to build a boat, show them the sea." (part 2)
>
> You do not necessarily have to appoint a project team member to take responsibility for a communication moment. Subsequent to dividing the individual tasks per communication moment, you can ask which project team member wants to take responsibility for a communication moment. Explain that with this responsibility also comes presenting the results of the subproject to stakeholders.
>
> Presenting the results to stakeholders is very appealing for project team members because it increases their visibility within the organization. This visibility is important for the I-marketing [5.4] of project team members, and that is why they will be eager to take responsibility for a communication moment.

In comparison to a traditional project plan, a process plan based on communication moments makes it much easier to delegate responsibility to project team members. This is because every subproject leads to a real presentation to a stakeholder. The time that you save by delegating responsibility, can be invested on coaching project team members. Help them to efficiently manage their subproject and to market the project [5.2] and the project team [5.3]. If the project team member is successful with a communication message, then the project team will also be perceived as successful. As a result, you will be perceived as successful because you are the leader of that project team [5.1].

As manager of the total project, you can successfully manage all these subprojects by constantly reverting to the action lists (Table 2). At each meeting with the project team, you have to assess whether the execution of the individual tasks for a communication moment is still on schedule. Subsequently, you have to determine whether all planned individual tasks, with the present understanding, will successfully *seduce* stakeholders into the change that you want to realize.

## 3.5 Make a U-turn

A powerful communication message to present on the first communication moment in your project is the process plan based on communication moments itself.

By presenting the process plan to for example internal users, you communicate what your project's ultimate goal is and via which process you are planning to reach this goal. This openness in the beginning of the project creates trust between internal users and you. You create trust because your process plan expresses that you will frequently communicate with them [3.1] during the project. By this, you let internal users know that their voice will be heard and that they will be able to exert influence on your advice to the client. As a result, internal users become involved early in the project, which contributes to successfully *seducing* them into change.

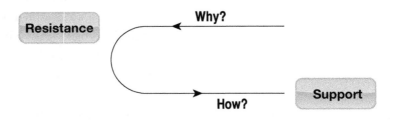

**Figure 8** U-turn from "why change" to "how to change"

The presentation of this process plan enables you to make a U-turn with internal users from "why change" to "how to change" (Figure 8). This U-turn is necessary because internal users initially tend to resist change (Appendix B). This resistance is traditionally caused by the fact that a too large psychological step is expected from internal users. They are expected to accept the "why" of the change simultaneously with a prescriptive description on "how" they have to change. Prescriptively describing which changes in attitude or working method you expect from internal users will evoke resistance because all that remains for the internal users is to follow what the project team has devised.

By presenting the process plan, you give internal users the opportunity to first get accustomed to the "why" of the change. As soon as they are convinced of the "why," then you can *seduce* them to think constructively on "how" to achieve this change. Consciously making this U-turn with internal users will create much more support and buy-in for the change that you want to realize.

This also holds true for other stakeholders in the political arena [2.3]. Presenting your process plan based on communication moments opens the "why" discussion early in the project. This creates an equal starting position for stakeholders. You level the playing field, which creates the trust that is necessary to realize a successful change.

> Presenting the process plan early in the project is sometimes perceived as a sign of weakness by internal consultants. It would give the impression that you as an internal consultant are uncertain about how to approach the project.
>
> The internal consultants, who have tried it, indicated that they experienced great benefits. Stakeholders are engaged early in the project, and by presenting the process plan, a minimally time-consuming first communication moment is created.
>
> Experience shows also that it considerably strengthens the team spirit. Celebrate with your project team when the process plan has been reviewed by the client, internal users, and other stakeholders in the political arena [2.3]. The project team has done a good job and the first step towards realizing a successful organizational change has been made.

## 3.6 Respect the Plan

A common known function of a traditional project plan is that it helps to efficiently organize project activities. An often overlooked second function is that it serves as a contract. This contract is traditionally concluded with the client and primarily presented to the client. This is because a traditional project plan is only interesting to the client.

Other stakeholders are often not interested in a list of milestones that are technically required to produce a solution. A process plan based on communication moments, however, is interesting to stakeholders because it describes when you will communicate with them.

This interest gives you the opportunity to virtually conclude a contract with more stakeholders than just the client. The advantage is that your control on the project dramatically increases.

It works in the same way as trying to quit smoking. If you do not tell anyone that you are going to quit, then it is easier to go back on your promise. However, if you share your intentions with family and friends, then the incentive is greater to quit. In other words, it is not only the plan that makes you successful, but also presenting that plan.

By presenting your process plan based on communication moments, you make it in fact a shared document. A shared document can only be changed if the stakeholders with whom the document is shared are informed. Stakeholders who need to be informed are the stakeholders who you consciously have selected in the political arena [2.3]. Exposure to bosses, direct colleagues, and other stakeholders in the political arena will prevent for example the client from radically altering the project while you are executing it.

In addition to a broad presentation of the process plan, also pre-planning the communication moments in the agendas of the stakeholders [3.2] brings you in control of your project. Pre-planning the communication moments creates "pressure cookers" in your project. This will stimulate stakeholders to make decisions in order to further progress.

Pre-planning the communication moments will significantly reduce delays in execution because a delay is traceable to a specific stakeholder. A stakeholder who has additional demands (scope creep) or is otherwise slowing down your project, becomes visible to other stakeholders because they can trace the culprit in the process plan based on communication moments.

This potential exposure to other stakeholders in the political arena will encourage a stakeholder to respect the plan with all its deadlines and agreed activities. As a consequence, a process plan based on communication moments has significantly more chance to be executed on time and on budget than a traditional project plan.

A process plan based on communication moments is not a static, but a dynamic contract. It is extremely flexible to use because each communication moment gives you the opportunity to assess with stakeholders if the desired result is still feasible. If reality demands a drastic change in the project, then the process plan can be adjusted. This revised plan should be communicated again to all important stakeholders. Additionally, this "restart" of your project gives you great flexibility in re-negotiating aspects like time, budget, and quality (iron triangle). In other words, you can set your new conditions based on a "known" situation, which will greatly enhance your chance on realizing a successful change.

# Organize
# Influence

*Jia-li is confronted with an overactive steering committee. The steering committee consists of the client, the client's manager, a board member, and the program director. Jia-li senses that the steering committee, instead of her, is managing the project. The steering committee does not only monitor deviations from the project plan, but it is also increasingly instructing Jia-li what to do. The steering committee is putting pressure on Jia-li to deliver results earlier than agreed upon. Furthermore, they are increasingly ignoring the interests of the internal users. The interests of the steering committee and those of the internal users are exponentially diverging. Jia-li fears that her project will implode. She wants to know what she can do to increase her influence in the steering committee in order to get in control of her project again.*

Every change project can greatly benefit from a steering committee, PIT team, project review board, project office, steering group, project governance team, commission, reference board, or project board. These so-called governance bodies can be used as vehicles to convey your ideas on how to realize a successful change. The third SPOMP strategy "Organize Influence" (Figure 9) shows how you can utilize such a body to *seduce* stakeholders into change. You will learn how you can organize your influence in such a way that the governance body starts working for you.

S = Select Your Stakeholders

P = Plan to Communicate

**O = Organize Influence**

M = Market Your Change Initiative

P = Prove Potential Success

**Figure 9** SPOMP strategy: Organize Influence

Traditionally, a governance body mainly consists of members representing the interests of the client's side. This has the advantage that you will secure executive support for the change that you want to realize. However, the disadvantage is that often a solution will be developed that primarily satisfies the needs of the client's side only. Such a solution is difficult to sell to other stakeholders in the political arena [2.0]. Therefore, you have to convince the client to include other stakeholders in the governance body.

At minimum, a representative of the internal users should be included in the governance body. This opens the opportunity for the client and the internal user(s) to discuss their different interests face-to-face.

The advantage for you is that you do not have to bridge the different interests between them anymore. The body members themselves will bridge the differences for you. Basically, body members will *seduce* each other into change, and then the governance body starts working for you [4.1].

In order to make maximum use of this governance body, you need to organize your influence. A powerful approach is to first make sure that the actual interests in the political arena are reflected in the body [4.2]. Subsequently, you need to determine which political powers you would like to include as a body member to voice these different interests [4.3]. By controlling who will be invited as a member, you will increase your influence because you can form strategic coalitions with these members. Finally, you can further increase your influence by balancing the political powers in the governance body [4.4]. Creating an optimum power balance gives you the latitude necessary to realize a successful organizational change.

## 4.1  Why a Governance Body

Without a governance body, you are in a one-to-one relationship with the client. As a consequence, you will be dependent on the client because he has more political power than you. Establishing a governance body dramatically improves your relative power balance with the client. This is because the client's power is distributed among the members of the governance body. These body members can be used to influence your client.

Establishing a governance body has many other advantages. Stakeholders, who are included as a member of this body, will feel engaged in the project and in the change that you wish to realize. Members will feel engaged because of the "information advantage" that you give them in comparison to other stakeholders who are not included in the body.

This information advantage means power, and in general, every stakeholder is sensitive to power. It will motivate them to contribute constructively to the project, and it will engage them to feel jointly responsible for the project's success. Stakeholders who feel engaged are much easier to *seduce* into the change you want to realize.

Stakeholders will also feel engaged because you feed their egos by inviting them to actively think along as body members. If, for example, you include someone from the compliance department to contribute in the development of a solution, then he will be more committed to successfully implement this solution. He will be more committed because you gave him the feeling that his opinion is valuable and is appreciated. This positive feeling makes it easier for you to *seduce* him to follow your lead.

Another advantage of establishing a governance body is that the members will bring realism to the expectations of the stakeholders whom they represent. Through discussions in the body, members will become aware that achieving an organizational change is a complex endeavor. Body members will inform stakeholders of this complexity. As a result, these represented stakeholders will get a more realistic view on what may be expected of the project. They will start to understand that not all of their wishes can be met. In other words, the expectations of these stakeholders are managed through their representatives in the governance body. This will make it easier for you to *seduce* stakeholders on a communication moment [3.0].

Finally, the advantage of establishing a governance body is that each meeting of this group offers you a unique opportunity to market the project, the project team, and your own role as the orchestrator of the change [5.0]. Also this helps you to *seduce* stakeholders into change.

You can let the governance body work for you, if you ensure that the actual interests in the political arena are reflected in the body [4.2].

Next to establishing a governance body, there are several other ways to actively engage stakeholders in the project. For example, you can organize a brainstorming session with certain stakeholders to prepare a particular part of the project. Alternatively, you can set up a pilot, where a number of internal users test a beta version or a group of managers who test the authorization procedure. Another option is to organize a lunch meeting with internal users or other interested stakeholders. You could also organize a contest for the most original solution to your project.

There are many ways to actively engage stakeholders in the change you want to realize. Think about it because the more stakeholders you give an active role in the project, the more commitment you will instill. This commitment is a prerequisite to successfully *seduce* stakeholders into the change that you want to realize.

## 4.2 Reflecting the Actual Political Interests

In the political arena [2.3] in which you have to realize change, a variety of interests often play a role. This variety of interests stems from a mix of wishes and anxieties that stakeholders have regarding your project and the change that you want to realize. As an internal consultant, you can bridge these different interests yourself on every communication moment [3.0], but a powerful strategy is also to delegate this task to the governance body.

A governance body starts working for you when you ensure that the interests to be discussed in the body are a simplified reflection of the interests that actually play a role in the political arena (Figure 10). Reflecting these actual political interests in the body is very powerful because it ensures that the most conflicting interests will be discussed in the body.

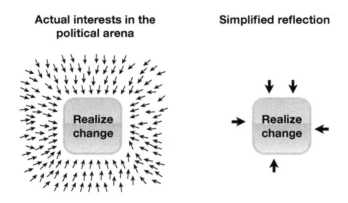

**Figure 10** Reflecting the actual political interests

If the interests discussed in the body reflect the actual political interests, then it becomes much easier for you to realize change at the project level. By discussing the conflicts of interest in the body, you will create

As an external strategy consultant, I often facilitated the purchasing, production, and sales departments to communicate with each other. The purchasing department is traditionally judged on purchasing products at a low cost, while the production department is judged on minimum loss and the quality of the end product. Obviously, this is difficult to achieve when the purchasing strategy is primarily driven by the purchase price.

Furthermore, the sales department is judged on the number of end products sold. In order to sell as much as possible, products are often sold more "positively" than what the production department can deliver.

By bringing the purchasing, production, and sales department heads together, you create mutual understanding for the conflicting interests in the business model. The notion of understanding each other's motives creates a common ground to address the problem and to work on the solution. Bringing together different interests in a governance body creates in the same way a common ground for change.

a common ground for change. In this way, it is not you who *seduces* stakeholders to bridge the different interests, but the different interests are bridged by the body members themselves. The governance body now starts working for you, and as a consequence you will be much more successful in creating support and buy-in for the change.

In the discussion amongst body members, the emphasis should not lie on the conflict of interests but on the search for opportunities and the willingness to create change together. You should encourage members to look beyond their own interests and inspire them to think about what is best for organization as a whole. To achieve this, you have to align your project with the organization's strategic mission.[6]

If the interests in the body reflect the actual political interests, then the pace with which your client wants to change becomes synchronized

---

[6] My next book "HR Strategic Project Management PLUS" (expected 2013/14) describes how you can align your project with the strategic mission of your organization. Other subjects covered in this upcoming book are presented on the last page of this book.

with the pace internal users can (or are willing to) change. The client often aims to implement a change as fast and as efficient as possible.

The internal users on the other hand, often pay more importance to a user-friendly and conscientious implementation. If the body reflects the actual political interests, then you do not need to monitor the "change-ability" of the organization anymore, as the body members will do so.

## 4.3 Form Strategic Coalitions

After you have decided which interests you would like to have discussed in the governance body [4.2], you should determine which individuals will be voicing these interests. You need to assess if the client is voicing his interests on his own, or if you want indirect clients [2.3.1] to support the client in his mission. Furthermore, you have to determine which stakeholders will be voicing the interests of the internal users' side [2.3.2] in the body.

Determining which stakeholders to include in the governance body significantly increases your influence in the body. First, you create for yourself the opportunity to include advocates of the intended change into the body. Advocates of the change can help you in the body meeting to eliminate potential resistance from other body members. Secondly, you create for yourself the opportunity to include the stakeholders with whom you can form a strategic coalition. By giving yourself this opportunity, you substantially enhance your power in the body.

You can strengthen your coalition by including a careershaper [2.3.5] in the body. This not only fosters your career [8.0], but also secures the availability of human resources for your project. With this careershaper, you can form a coalition if, for example, the client and/or internal users start making unrealistic demands regarding your project.

Finally, you can strengthen your coalition by including a favorable secondary stakeholder [2.3.3] or an ambassador [2.3.4] as a body member. By forming a coalition with these stakeholders, you empower yourself to steer the decision-making process of the body. If you can steer this process, then the governance body is working for you.

Once you have decided which stakeholders will be voicing the different interests in the governance body, you need to optimize the power balance in the body [4.4]. Optimizing the power balance is essential when you want to make maximum use of the governance body.

## 4.4  Optimize the Power Balance

To use the political forces in the governance body to your advantage, you need to optimize the power balance. Your influence in the body is theoretically at its maximum when the power between the client's side and the internal users' side are in balance. When this power balance exists, you basically only need to join a side in order to influence the decision-making process of the body. This theoretical power balance gives you latitude to develop a solution to which both sides can be *seduced*.

In practice, the client's side often has the most political power in the governance body. This power is needed in order to change the organization. The power of the client's side must always be larger than the resistance you anticipate from other stakeholders when changing the organization. If you expect that the resistance is larger, then you will have to increase the power of the client's side. You can increase this power by including an additional board member or another indirect client [2.3.1] with sufficient formal power (Figure 11A).

If you do not succeed in increasing the power of the client's side, then it is not likely that the organizational or behavioral change will be realized. In this case, it is better to decline the project assignment because you always need a sufficiently powerful client's side to reach the upper limit of the organization's changeability.

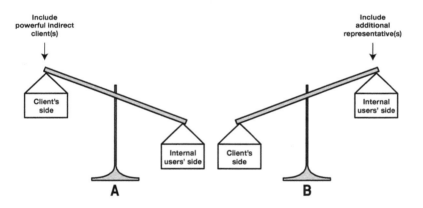

**Figure 11** Optimizing the power balance

The power of the client's side must therefore be large enough to successfully achieve change in the organization, but it must not be too large. If the client's side has too much power in the body, then the interests of the other stakeholders will be voted out. As a result, you will have to create support within the organization for a viewpoint that is predominantly formulated by the client's side. This results in a push-strategy, where the change can only be realized by hierarchically enforcing it. Many organizational and behavioral change projects fail due to the fact that the client's side has too much power and is coercing other stakeholders into change (Appendix A).

In order to create the optimal power balance for your project, you need to increase the power of the internal users' side, simply because you cannot decrease the power of the client's side.

The easiest way to do so is to include an additional representative(s) of the internal users' side in the governance body (Figure 11B). In practice, this is not always desirable when, for example, politically sensitive subjects like economy measures are being discussed in the body. In this case, a powerful strategy is to establish a second body next to the existing governance body [4.5], called a "soundboard group" (or advisory board). In this soundboard group, you can now include representatives of the internal users' side so as to secure "user involvement" (Appendix A). In addition, you can decide to include other stakeholders of the political arena whose interests are not yet represented.

## 4.5 Managing Bodies

If you decide to establish two bodies, then one body often consists of representatives of the client's side (traditional governance body), while in the other body the interests of the internal users' side are represented (soundboard group). It is recommendable to let the client bridge the gap between these bodies.

In order to let the client bridge the gap, you have to make sure that the client speaks on behalf of the traditional governance body within the soundboard group and on behalf of the soundboard group within the traditional governance body.

It is of strategic importance to delegate this (linking pin) role to the client. By delegating this role, you let politics between the bodies work for you. This additional responsibility for the client also ensures that you and the client will work closely together in approaching both bodies.

> Sometimes a project demands that the members of the soundboard group should be able to speak freely in their body meeting. This is true when a politically sensitive subject like layoffs needs to be discussed. In these cases, it is better not to delegate the bridging role between the two bodies to the client. Presence of the client in the soundboard group may disrupt discussions, and that is why it is sometimes recommendable that you take responsibility for the bridging role. Depending on the project and the situation, you have to decide whether it is better for you to take responsibility or that you delegate this responsibility to the client.

You will have to convince the client that either including an internal user in the governance body or establishing a soundboard group is an absolute prerequisite to a successful project. Eventually, the client will also acknowledge that the involvement of internal users is needed in order to realize a successful organizational change. As an unsuccessful project also radiates on the client, it is of interest to both of you to organize the influence of the internal users' side.

> Keep in mind that the client may be hesitant to involve the internal users' side. This is because more influence of the internal users will decrease the client's influence on the project. My next book "HR Strategic Project Management PLUS" (expected 2013/14) describes how you can compensate for this loss of influence that the client may experience. Other subjects covered in this upcoming book are presented on the last page of this book.

# Market Your
# Change Initiative

*Rafael and his team find themselves caught in a stalemate. The client, internal users, and other stakeholders all have different opinions about the project. The client wants to finish the project as soon as possible because he needs Rafael for another project. The client's management sees Rafael's project as a part of a larger transition and wants to extend the scope of the project. The internal users, on the other hand, tend to opt for a scenario which ensures a smooth implementation of the proposed organizational change. However, this scenario will increase the project duration. Rafael and his team developed a plan to get out of this stalemate, but it requires extra funds from an indecisive finance manager. Rafael's team has communicated the benefits of this plan to the stakeholders concerned, but is having difficulty convincing them. Rafael wants to learn how he can sell his change initiative to these stakeholders in order to seduce them into a successful change.*

Your solution, change strategy, or plan on how to implement change has to align with the organization's strategic agenda and is therefore not always what the client, internal users, or other stakeholders may have hoped for. That is why you need to sell your change initiative to stakeholders. Actively selling the change that you recommend is necessary because change is in principle undesirable for a portion of the stakeholders (Appendix B).

The fourth SPOMP strategy "Market Your Change Initiative" (Figure 12) deploys marketing techniques to help you sell the desired change to stakeholders. Unfortunately, in traditional project and change management literature, there is almost no consideration given to the powerful role of marketing in realizing change.

S = Select Your Stakeholders

P = Plan to Communicate

O = Organize Influence

**M = Market Your Change Initiative**

P = Prove Potential Success

**Figure 12** SPOMP strategy: Market Your Change Initiative

You can sell an organizational change by making it desirable for stakeholders. In order to do so, you need to influence the perception that stakeholders have of the change. This perception is a subjective observation (cognitive impression) of reality. If you are able to give stakeholders a positive perception of your project (and of the people behind it), then they will be more susceptible to support your ideas. In that way, it becomes much easier to *seduce* them into the change you want to realize.

Positively influencing the perception is actually also what a manufacturer does to sell his product. He influences the customer's perception by marketing his product. This marketing effort is only effective when the communication message is communicated frequently to the potential customer, just like a television commercial. That is why it is crucial to have multiple communication moments [3.0] in your project. Every communication moment gives you "air time" to broadcast your communication message to continuously influence the perception of stakeholders.

You can make the perception of change positive by influencing the stakeholder on three levels [5.1]. You need to create trust in the project [5.2], the project team [5.3], and in yourself as the orchestrator of the change [5.4]. Only if stakeholders gain trust at all three levels, it will become possible to *seduce* them to exchange the current (safe) way of working for the new (uncertain) way you recommend. Therefore, all three levels have to be consistently promoted at each communication moment. Helpful tools to do so include creating your own logo [5.5] and to "pimp" your communication message [5.6] in order to make the change more attractive to stakeholders.

Marketing involves the arousal of trust. Manufacturers advertise their products for this reason. Using advertising, manufacturers try to convince the customer that their branded product is of better quality then an unbranded product and that a higher price is justified because of this quality. However, almost no customer really knows whether the branded product is of better quality. It is only occasionally disproved by a comparison test performed by a consumer organization. Just as manufacturers use marketing to *seduce* the customer, you can deploy marketing to *seduce* stakeholders into the change you want to realize.

# 5.1 Relationship between Project-, Team-, and I-marketing

Stakeholders can only be *seduced* into change if they have a positive perception of the change that you want to realize. Therefore, it is imperative to communicate positively about the project at every communication moment (project marketing). This means, for example, to convince stakeholders that your approach to the project is the right one [5.2].

In addition, you have to communicate positively about the project team at every communication moment (team marketing). Explain which qualities each project team member possesses and what positive influence this has on the change that you want to realize [5.3].

Lastly, you have to communicate positively about your own role at every communication moment (I-marketing), by convincing stakeholders that you are the right person to successfully manage this change [5.4].

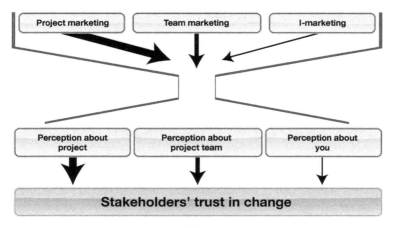

**Figure 13** Stakeholders' trust is mainly impacted by project marketing

If trust is lacking at one of the three levels (Figure 13), it will become difficult to *seduce* stakeholders into change. For example, if the project team is perceived as mediocre, then stakeholders will have little trust in the quality of the project and will not put much value on the output of the project team. As a consequence, communicating the advantages that your project holds for the organization will not be received well. In this case, stakeholders will not be *seduced* into the intended change.

The same is applicable to you as manager of the change project. If stakeholders have the perception that the project team is led by an average project manager, then they will have little trust in the project's progress. In that case stakeholders have a negative perception, and this will foster resistance.

In other words, you will have to influence the stakeholders' perception at all three levels in order to create trust. Relatively speaking, most consideration in this respect should be given to the project marketing because by promoting your project, you automatically promote the project team and yourself (Figure 13).

Think about what makes you choose to watch a particular movie. The title is not the only factor on which you decide to go see a movie. Your choice is also based on the name of the producer, director, actors, movie company, type of theater, advertising in the newspaper, and the number of weeks that the movie is running.

Your decision-making process is influenced by many factors. Also, for projects it is important to consciously give consideration to the factors that influence the stakeholders' decision-making. That is why you should not only market your project but also the team behind it.

## 5.2 Project Marketing

Project marketing means that you communicate positively about the project and the change you want to realize. The aim is to positively influence stakeholders that the project will lead to a better functioning organization.

First, you can create a positive perception by presenting stakeholders your process plan based on communication moments [3.5]. By presenting this process plan, you show stakeholders how you are going to approach the project and that you have no hidden agenda. The communication moments [3.2] in your process plan indicate to stakeholders that at set times they will be listened to. This arouses trust and leaves the stakeholders with a positive perception of your project.

Secondly, a positive perception can be created by showing stakeholders that you are making the progress that you had anticipated in the process plan. In a traditional progress report, you show which project activities you have executed and which activities are still planned to be executed. Bear in mind that this retrospective character of a traditional progress report is only of partial interest to stakeholders. Above all, stakeholders need information about the advancement being made in changing the attitude of people in the organization. Therefore, it is much more effective to prove the potential success of your project [6.0]. This means that you will prove to stakeholders that your project has the potential to realize a beneficial organizational change. Proclaiming the potential success of your project leads others to participate in the project. This is because people consciously, but also often subconsciously, want to join a winning team.

Lastly, you can create a positive perception by voicing at every communication moment the amount of support and buy-in that you have from stakeholders. In this respect, proclaiming the support from the client's side [2.3.1] and the internal users' side [2.3.2] has the most impact (Appendix A).

## 5.3 Team Marketing

Team marketing means promoting the project team that is responsible for realizing the intended change. If the perception exists that the project team is capable, then this automatically creates trust amongst stakeholders in the outcome of the project.

In order to create this positive perception of the project team, it is important to introduce each member of the team to the stakeholders at an early stage in the project. In doing so, you should explain which qualities each team member possesses and how the specific composition of the project team will contribute to a successful

In this respect, imagine a kidnapping case. The president of the country announces that the best elite team has been assigned to it. The leader of the elite team has 20 years of experience and has resolved almost every kidnapping case successfully. Also, each team member is the absolute specialist in his field.

Many of us will have trust in the successful resolution of this kidnapping case. Every kidnapping case is of course totally different, but still we have this trust. We have trust because prior to the kidnapping case, we are introduced to the competencies of the team members. This prior information creates a positive perception and trust in a successful resolution.

change. Introducing project team members creates trust, which will stimulate the *seduction* of stakeholders into change.

Team marketing also means that you have to consciously communicate about the good cooperation, atmosphere, and the professionalism within the project team. Communication moments [3.0] are particularly suited to this, but you can also promote your project team at other meetings. By consciously proclaiming the quality of the project team, you create a positive perception amongst stakeholders. This creates trust in the project team and therefore trust in the project and in yourself as the leader of that team.

Besides building a closely-knit project team, team marketing also ensures that the project team members want to exert themselves with regard to the project. They will want to exert themselves because promoting the project team creates a shared feeling of responsibility. If the project fails, then this will also affect the image of each individual member of the team. As a result, each project team member will be intrinsically motivated to make a success of the project.

## 5.4 I-marketing

I-marketing is promoting your own role as the leader of the project team and the orchestrator of the change. Therefore, you have to express that you want to deliver a quality project and that you are serious in taking on responsibility for the project. You have to show that you do not just want to deliver a solution "for the bookshelf," but that you genuinely want to improve the organization and are perseverant in successfully reaching that goal.

Make sure that you always deliver on the agreed communication moments [3.0]. By delivering precisely on time, you actually show that you have everything completely under control. This creates trust that the project is in good hands with you.

Self-promotion makes many people feel uneasy. This uneasy feeling is misplaced because it is not about exaggerating your capabilities, but rather showing what your capabilities are. By showing your capabilities, you create trust. That is why I-marketing is a crucial factor in positively influencing the perception.

For example, you as a reader have maybe acquired "HR Strategic Project Management SPOMP" because you want to manage even more interesting projects in the future, or to further your career. However, would you have acquired this book if it had been written by someone with no experience in managing complex projects? Probably not. My extensive experience as a change manager and coach gave you the trust to acquire this book. Explicitly mentioning my credentials on the backside of this book gave you the perception that this book comprises valuable information and that it was a good investment in your career.

Of course, I could have counted on the fact that the reader would become convinced of the quality of this book whilst reading it. It goes without saying that I have every trust in that, but I-marketing makes it a little easier for me to sell the book, just as I-marketing will make it easier for you to sell the change that you want to realize.

On every communication moment, you have to emphasize that your project is successful [5.2] and that a highly capable project team is working on it [5.3]. By communicating positively about the project, the perception of a successful project team is generated. You are a part of this project team. So, by emphasizing the quality of the project and the project team, you are indirectly promoting your own role as the orchestrator of the change.

I-marketing is more subtle than just trumpeting your horn. You have to stimulate others to communicate positively about your merits as an internal consultant. Promoting project team members is one way of doing so because you incite them to promote you in turn.

Another way is to create ambassadors [2.3.4] for your project. Ambassadors convey the success of the project. The recipient of this message will then conclude that a good project team is working on it under the leadership of a capable project manager.

Also the third SPOMP strategy "Organize Influence" [4.0] offers you opportunities for self-promotion. The efficient and effective way you prepare and organize the body meetings, will positively influence the perception of your role as a professional. That is why it is important to include a careershaper [2.3.5] in the governance body.

Interviewing internal users, negotiating with the client,[7] consulting experts and colleagues, conducting a survey, . . . for each interaction it is important to leave a positive impression of your project and the quality of your project team members. The more your team gets itself onto the map, the more I-marketing for you. A helpful tool that contributes in this respect is to create your own logo [5.5]. Alongside that you can "pimp" your communication message in order to make the change more attractive to stakeholders [5.6].

---

[7] My next book "HR Strategic Project Management PLUS" (expected 2013/14) describes how you can create a strong negotiating position towards the client. Other subjects covered in this upcoming book are presented on the last page of this book.

## 5.5 Create Your Own Logo

A process plan based on communication moments offers an excellent platform to make your efforts as a project team visible. In order to increase this visibility, you have to ensure that the products or communication messages [3.2] that you produce are recognizable to the stakeholders. A recognizable product in fact creates a positive perception. That is why people tend to choose a familiar product over an unknown product.

For this reason, it is recommendable that every communication message contains something unique: a project logo. When your report, presentation, or other communication messages are viewed, every stakeholder should instantly think of your project. At a minimum, a logo consists of the title of the project. Try to make a distinguishing title that sticks. For example, "Payroll system 2.0" sticks better in the memory than "A first survey of new Payroll system."

A logo can also include an image that illustrates your project or the layout that you use in presentations or reports. Try developing a logo that not only makes your project stand out qualitatively, but also visually. Stakeholders will then recognize the origin, which will support your team marketing [5.3].

Lastly, you can consider developing a logo for yourself as internal consultant. From this logo, stakeholders should recognize that you are responsible, and this supports your I-marketing [5.4]. Your personal logo should always be more subtle than the project logo because ultimately you are judged upon the projects that you manage.

Organizations often have their own (corporate) format for the definitive advisory report. This format offers you little possibility to introduce something unique, something distinguishing. However, for concepts, surveys, project plans, memos, presentations, and other intermediate communication messages, there is often room to introduce your own logo.

For example, I led a knowledge management project for which the project logo was a depiction of the Nile Delta. Everyone who saw our products recognized its origin immediately. Furthermore, I often use a personal logo for the intermediate products that I produce — a horizontal gray bar as a header over the entire page, containing the project title. Stakeholders, therefore, will recognize what was produced on my responsibility.

# 5.6 "Pimp" Your Communication Message

For the presentation of a new book or CD, often a release party is organized. The aim is to draw attention and create a positive perception of the product. Pimping your communication message means that you draw attention to your project by giving consideration to the "packaging" of your change message. The goal is to make it more attractive to stakeholders in order to *seduce* them into change.

There are many ways to pimp your communication message. For example, you can hand over the advisory report to the president of your organization and have a photograph taken of it. This photograph can be used to promote your project in an article on the intranet or in your organization's staff magazine. The attention that you draw creates a positive perception, which will contribute to your project-, team-, and I-marketing [5.1].

Another way of pimping your communication message is to present the data gathered by your project team more attractively. Try to visualize data as much as possible through an illustration, figure, or table. Consider presenting the results of a survey in an infographic, the project's progress in a bar chart, or a bar chart representing how far other organizations are progressing on the same subject. Keep in mind that a graphic representation is often better remembered by stakeholders and therefore contributes to positively influencing the perception.

Besides the graphic visualization of data, you can also pimp your communication message by adding suggestive information. This means that you generate soft or cosmetic data in order to color the perception of the recipient. The following figure illustrates an example of how cosmetic data can influence the perception.

**Figure 14**  Example of pimping my book

Figure 14 describes how often this book refers to a certain paragraph. In fact, this says nothing about the quality of each paragraph. Still, this suggestive information will create the perception that the paragraph called "process plan based on communication moments" is a very important paragraph in this book.

In conclusion, pimping your communication message is a very important element in order to market your change initiative. Remember that not only the intrinsic quality of your solution is important, but also how it is perceived. So, with your team, think about how you can positively influence this perception by making the change more attractive to the recipient.

# Prove
# Potential Success

*Maura and her team have analyzed the political arena and organized several communication moments in the project. On each communication moment, she is planning to positively influence the stakeholders' perception by marketing the project, the project team, and herself. However, Maura experiences difficulties to market her project. The benefits of the intended change for the organization as a whole are clear, but how can she seduce an individual stakeholder? How can she provide proof to stakeholders during the project that a successful change will be realized? A complicating factor is also that the perception of a successful change differs per stakeholder. So how can Maura prove that her project will be successful for each and every stakeholder?*

The fifth and final SPOMP strategy "Prove Potential Success" (Figure 15) helps to prove the success of your project, while executing it. Proving this "potential" success is extremely powerful because it gives you the proverbial "carrot" to *seduce* stakeholders into change [6.1].

S = Select Your Stakeholders

P = Plan to Communicate

O = Organize Influence

M = Market Your Change Initiative

**P = Prove Potential Success**

**Figure 15** SPOMP strategy: Prove Potential Success

Proving potential success means gathering proof that your project will be successful in realizing a beneficial change for each and every stakeholder. Presenting this proof on a communication moment [3.0] will help you to *seduce* the client, internal users, and other stakeholders.

In order to prove this potential success, you will need indicators on which you can assess success [6.2]. A practical approach to identify these potential success indicators is to brainstorm with your project team and to ask stakeholders [6.3].

The indicators need to be quantitative [6.4] because you want to be able to measure them. Measuring the value of these indicators at different moments in your project makes the advancement in the organizational change process visible. By demonstrating this advancement on communication moments, you prove the potential success of your project to stakeholders.

The mix of indicators that you are going to use to prove the potential success form together a sophisticated instrument. This instrument empowers you to anticipate unexpected developments in your project and to manage potential project risks much more effectively [6.5].

This chapter concludes with a technique that is called "spinning the context" [6.6]. This technique, often used by spin doctors, will indirectly influence the stakeholders' perception of the potential success that you are going to present.

> Proving potential success is basically what a politician does to convince voters of his political program or what environmental organizations do to convince people. The true success of the proposed program is only measurable after many years. Politicians and environmentalists sell their ideas by proving the potential success of their programs. Likewise, you can sell your project by proving its potential success.

## 6.1 The Power of Potential Success

The advantage of proving potential success during the project is that stakeholders will gain trust in a good project close-out. They will start to "believe" in the project and in you as the orchestrator of the change, which will make it much easier to *seduce* stakeholders.

A second advantage is that stakeholders will get the impression that the organizational change process is already advancing. Proving potential success will create the perception that the "train" is in motion and that stakeholders should jump onto it now if they want to be able to influence the outcome. This willingness to act that you create is a precondition to *seduce* stakeholders to change from the current to the new way of working.

Third, proving potential success has the effect of attracting stakeholders. People simply do like to join in with a project when other people are talking about its success. You create a winning atmosphere because everyone wants to identify, consciously or subconsciously, with success.

Fourth, proving potential success ensures that the stakeholders' expectations are managed with respect to the end result of your project. If the presented potential success on a communication moment [3.0] does not meet their expectations, these expectations will get adjusted during the project. Of course, it is also possible that the expectations with respect to the end result remain the same. In that case, stakeholders in the political arena [2.0] could put pressure on the client to make extra resources available, or, in the worst case, to replace you as the person responsible.

A last advantage is that the project team becomes much more motivated. By presenting the potential success at a communication moment, members of the project team will see the results of their exertions. This enhances their "belief" in the project and will inspire them to go the "extra mile."

## 6.2 Fundamental Concept

Proving potential success means that you present proof at certain moments in the project that your project is on time, on budget, and is en route to reach the project's end goal (the organizational change that you want to realize).

Suppose that your department's resources are burdened by frequent telephone consults from employees in your organization. Most answers can be found on the HR intranet, but employees apparently prefer to speak to a HR representative for information. Your project assignment is to *seduce* these employees (internal users) to change their behavior. You want them to consult the information on the HR intranet first, before picking up the telephone. You define together with your client the end goal of your project as: Reduce the number of telephone consults to the HR department by 20 percent within 12 months (for simplicity reasons, budget being left out of the equation).

The indicator on which you will evaluate your project's success after 12 months is "the number of telephone consults." However, this indicator can also be used to prove the potential success during the project (Figure 16).

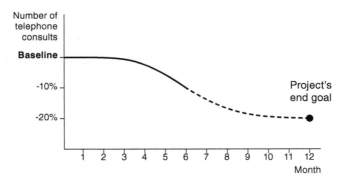

**Figure 16** Fundamental concept to prove potential success

Suppose that you measure this indicator in month 6 of your project and that the result of this measurement reveals 10 percent fewer telephone consults to the HR department. This intermediate result proves that you are en route to reach the project's end goal. By presenting this result at a communication moment [3.0] to the client, he will gain trust in the remaining six months of your project. In other words, measuring this indicator proves the potential success of your project to the client.

Presenting this result to the internal users and other stakeholders also proves to them the potential success of your project. It shows them that the project team's efforts have impact and that there is motion towards the end goal of the project.

The above described method is the fundamental concept to prove the potential success of your project. In short, you need to identify indicators [6.3] that you can measure at different moments in your project in order to prove the advancement in the organizational change process.

The first moment that you measure an indicator is called a baseline measurement. This baseline measurement needs to be established at an early stage in the project because you want to be able to prove a value change on that indicator as a result of your efforts. In this way, you prove the potential success of your project.

## 6.3 Indicators of Success

Obviously, the previous example [6.2] is oversimplified. A significant change on the indicator "number of telephone consults to the HR department" usually only occurs after your solution is implemented in the organization. Still, proving the potential success during your project will significantly ease the process of *seducing* stakeholders into change.

The challenge is to prove potential success as early as possible in the project. Because the earlier you can present proof, the more you can benefit from its positive effect in the remainder of the project.

Consider, for example, measuring the indicator "number of visitors to the HR intranet" during your project. The value of this indicator will increase when you are executing your project based on communication moments [3.0].

This increase is caused by the attention that you cultivate for your project. Presenting your process plan based on a communication moment [3.5] will make internal users curious about the content of the HR intranet pages and will encourage them to have a look at it. The increased number of visitors that you will measure as a result proves to the client that your project is potentially successful. This is because an increase presumably predicts fewer telephone consults to the HR department in the future.

> By planning your project on communication moments, you will produce frequent output through the communication messages that you present to stakeholders. This will create the perception that the project team is working effectively and efficiently. So by executing your process plan based on communication moments, you actually are positively influencing the stakeholders' perception of potential success during the project.

The previous example [6.2] is also oversimplified because in practice, stakeholders have different perceptions of the project's success. Bluntly put, internal users just want to have their HR questions answered. Indicators like "number of telephone consults" and "number of visitors to the HR intranet" do positively influence their perception about your project, but you will need to identify additional indicators in order to fully convince them of the potential success of your project. For instance, think of indicators that measure the user-friendliness of the HR intranet.

The key is to identify indicators that are easy to measure and apply to multiple stakeholders. To identify such indicators, brainstorm with your project team [6.3.1] about which indicators could prove the potential success to stakeholders. The indicators that you identify should be presented to the client, internal users, and other stakeholders in order to trigger a response. Presenting these indicators also offers a convenient opportunity to ask stakeholders [6.3.2] how they think the potential success during your project can be proved.

## 6.3.1 Identify Indicators with Your Project Team

In practice, four approaches are very powerful when brainstorming with your project team to identify potential success indicators (Figure 17).

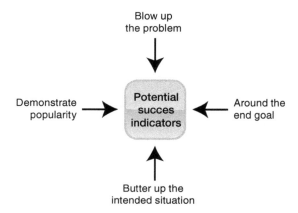

**Figure 17** Four approaches to identify potential success indicators with your project team

## Blow Up the Problem

A first approach to identify indicators is to "blow up the problem." This means that you brainstorm with your project team about indicators that accentuate the problem in the current situation (actual situation). For example, encourage your project team to search for data and statistics that explain what will happen if your project is not executed.

Blowing up the problem creates a sense of urgency and will stimulate the willingness to act. This willingness to act needs to be cultivated in order to *seduce* stakeholder to exchange the current situation for the intended situation (target situation).

The indicators that you use to blow up the problem can also be used to prove the potential success of your project. For instance, to identify potential success indicators for a Talent Management strategy, you can use the indicators "percentage of talents in your organization" and "percentage of talents internally promoted." By measuring the value of these indicators in previous years (Figure 18), you can stress the need for a Talent Management strategy. Extrapolating this trend to the future creates an urgency to change.

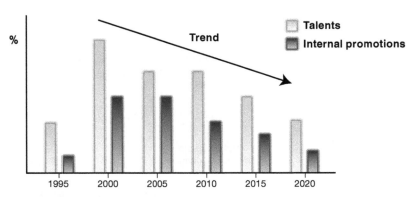

**Figure 18** "Blow up the problem" by extrapolation

Also, external sources can be used to blow up the problem. For example, you can substantiate the need for a Talent Management strategy by:

- Comparing the average percentage of talents in your organization with the industry average
- Using metrics about the "War for Talent"
- Comparing the retention rate in similar organizations

The use of industry and (inter)national benchmarks is a very potent way to blow up the problem. Moreover, these benchmarks represent indicators that you can use within your own organization in order to prove the potential success of your project.

**Around the End Goal**
A second approach to identify potential success indicators is to brainstorm with your project team about indicators around the project's end goal. Inspire your project team to not only look at the end goal that is defined with the client but to have a broader view. For example, anticipate what internal users and other stakeholders want to get out of the project and capture this in indicators. Do not only think in the short term but also in the longer term, such as alignment with the organization's strategic mission.

Inspire your project team to view things from a stakeholders' perspective. For example, ask project team members to think what kind of potential success your client needs in order to convince his boss of the project. Think broadly when brainstorming for potential success indicators per stakeholder, but always keep the project's end goal in mind.

Your assignment is to increase the turnover of the sales department by 10 percent within 12 months. This increased sales turnover is the indicator on which your project's success will be evaluated at completion.

Brainstorming with your project team around this end goal delivers indicators with which you can prove the potential success of this project. For example, the indicator "number of customer visits per month made by sales managers" can predict reaching your project's end goal. Suppose that in the beginning of your project this indicator measured on average 5.0 visits per month (baseline measurement). At a later stage in your project (for instance three months later), this indicator measures a result of 5.2 visits per month. This proves to stakeholders that the activity of sales managers has increased due to your project.

The effect that you prove with this indicator says nothing about realizing the actual aim of the project (10 percent increase in sales turnover). But still your project will be perceived as potentially successful by stakeholders. You positively influence the perception, because within three months you already present a visible improvement on an indicator (four percent more visits per month). This intermediate result creates trust for the remaining nine months of your project and therefore proves the potential success at this very moment.

## Butter Up the Intended Situation

A third approach to identify potential success indicators is to brainstorm with your project team on how to "butter up the intended situation." By making the intended situation more appealing to stakeholders, you create a willingness to change. This proves the potential success to stakeholders. Think in this respect of indicators that measure future benefits for a stakeholder:

- Less repetitive work
- Better monitoring and control opportunities
- Safer working environment

**Demonstrate Popularity**

A fourth and last approach is to identify indicators that demonstrate the popularity of your project. When you can prove that ever more people support and endorse your project, it will *seduce* others to follow and join in, too (bandwagon effect or herd behavior).

For example, think of the indicator "number of participants" at a workshop that you have organized. Or think of the presence of top management at the kick-off meeting of your project. You could also think of the go-ahead way your project is progressing in comparison with other organizations that are struggling with a similar problem.

Demonstrating the popularity of your project will create the perception that the project must be successful. This is because you are sharing that other stakeholders consider the project successful. If you can demonstrate during the project that the popularity is increasing (for example there were 30 percent more participants), then you will *seduce* stakeholders to fall in line with the growing number of supporters of your project (peer pressure).

> A commonly practiced approach to demonstrate popularity is the employee or stakeholder satisfaction survey. The indicator on which you measure success is satisfaction. If the value of this indicator is above a certain threshold, you have proved the potential success of your project.

## 6.3.2 Ask Stakeholders

Besides identifying potential success indicators with your project team [6.3.1], you should also consult stakeholders. Ask stakeholders how you can prove the potential success to them. Also, ask them to illustrate when they consider the end goal of your project successful.

You already know when the client considers your project successful. From the moment he assigned you to the project, he specified the end goal of the project and at which date this end goal is to be achieved.[8] Ask your client how you can prove during the project whether you are advancing in the right direction and at the right speed. Also, ask him what proof he needs in order to become convinced of the potential success of your project. In other words, get the client to collaborate in identifying indicators that can prove the potential success of your project.

By asking the same questions to internal users and other stakeholders, they will express their wishes or anxieties with regard to your project and the intended change (Table 3). From this response, you can derive many indicators of potential success. You will be positively amazed how many indicators are generated by such an exchange of thoughts. The advantage of asking stakeholders is that you gather potential success indicators in which stakeholders are interested. By meeting the stakeholders' expectations on a certain indicator, you have proved the potential success to that stakeholder.

You could measure, for example, the last indicator of Table 3 by testing a beta version of the user manual with a small group of internal users. If these internal users positively value this beta version, then you have

---

[8] My next book "HR Strategic Project Management PLUS" (expected 2013/14) describes how you can distill the actual project goal concealed in the initial project assignment. Other subjects covered in this upcoming book are presented on the last page of this book.

proved the potential success of your project to them. You can also prove the potential success to other internal users and stakeholders by presenting this positive response at a communication moment [3.0].

**Table 3** Examples of indicators that are derived from the internal users' wishes or anxieties

| Wish or Anxiety | Indicator |
| --- | --- |
| The application should not lead to extra red tape | Duration to fill in the application form |
| I find the project potentially successful if the management agrees to stick with the outcome of the project | Prove that management accepts outcome |
| The project team should provide a clear user manual in order to facilitate implementation | Satisfaction about user manual |

The stakeholder who expressed his anxiety about the red tape (Table 3) will consider your project potentially successful if you can prove that the new application form is less time-consuming than the previous one. This proof can also be used to positively influence other stakeholders.

Besides capturing wishes or anxieties in indicators, you can also identify indicators by asking stakeholders what kind of problems they currently experience (in the situation prior to your project). By doing so, you convey to stakeholders that their problem is taken seriously and that you are actively working on a solution. This creates a sense of urgency and stimulates a willingness to act. By accentuating the disadvantages of the current situation, you will influence stakeholders to favor change.

Questions to ask stakeholders in order to derive potential success indicators from the problem are for instance:

- What are the advantages and disadvantages with respect to the current situation?

- Which savings will be missed out on if nothing is done about the problem?
- Which penalties or measures threaten if, for example, a federal law is not implemented?

In practice, internal users often do not recognize the benefits or savings in the beginning of the project. However, by asking them, you do put the question in the internal users' minds. By that you create the need for an answer; because generally one wants to have a question answered. The response of the internal users can be used to urge your client to substantiate the "why" of the change [3.5]. Presenting the explanation of the client as to why your project is important now fulfills a need of the internal users and therefore proves the potential success to them.

In summary, ask stakeholders what they generally think of the project, the process plan, and of you as the orchestrator of the change. Moreover, ask their perception on the end goal of the project (that you have defined with your client) and their points of interest during the project's execution. Later in the project, ask their thoughts on the suggested solutions. You can derive many indicators of potential success from the stakeholders' responses to such questions. Because it is the stakeholder himself who has suggested these indicators, you learn how your efforts will be assessed. This knowledge helps you to lead your project (and the project team) more effectively. Being a successful project or change manager will then become a self-fulfilling prophecy.

## 6.4 Quantifying Indicators

In order to "prove" the potential success of your project, you need to be able to measure the identified indicators. A method to make qualitative indicators quantitative is to set up a Likert scale (Table 4).

**Table 4** Quantifying indicators with a Likert scale

|  | Disagree | | | Agree | |
|---|---|---|---|---|---|
|  | 1 | 2 | 3 | 4 | 5 |
| Over 50 percent of our employees are talented | O | O | O | O | O |
| We have to treat talents different from normal employees | O | O | O | O | O |

Suppose the stakeholders' response on the statements mentioned in Table 4 averages a score of respectively 4.3 and 2.3. The accuracy of this measurement is of minor importance. The aim is to re-measure these indicators during the project (ask response on both statements again) so as to demonstrate a value change with which you can prove potential success.

Another example is an employee satisfaction survey, where an average of 3.6 is scored on a five-point scale. This is the first time that you measure this indicator, so it is your baseline measurement. After three months, the survey returns an average score of 4.0. This is an increase of 11 percent compared to the baseline measurement.

The project assignment could also have been that you have to increase employee satisfaction by 15 percent. If the baseline measurement had a score of 2.7, then you have to demonstrate at least a score of 3.1 (2.7 × 1.15) at the project's completion. If you had a baseline measurement of 3.5, then your subsequent survey should return a minimum of 4.0

(3.5 × 1.15). In other words, the accuracy of the baseline measurement is less important. It is important, however, to keep the measuring method the same at each measurement moment. The change in value measured between the two moments is an indication of the potential success of your project.

Do not ponder whether a second measurement of an indicator will show a positive change. Measuring an indicator for the second time creates attention for an underlying problem. This attention alone already positively influences the perception of stakeholders (placebo effect). As a consequence the second measurement is often more favorable to your project than the previous one.

A "spider chart" can help to visualize how the value of an indicator has changed due to your project team's efforts. The figure below shows that stakeholders were hardly aware of the problem in the beginning of the project.

After presenting the process plan, this awareness greatly increased. By presenting this spider chart to stakeholders, you will positively influence their perception about your project and the change that you want to realize.

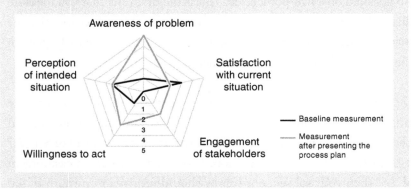

# 6.5 Effective Risk Management

Which indicators you need to select in order to prove potential success depends on the complexity of your project and the political arena [2.0] in which you are going to realize change. Selecting the right indicators is always an intellectually challenging task. Measuring too many indicators will affect efficiency within the project. Too few indicators will bring along the risk of not being credible for each and every stakeholder. Therefore, you should carefully choose which indicators to use in order to prove potential success.

The mix of indicators that you use to prove the potential success of your project form together a sophisticated instrument. Figuratively speaking, the instrument does not only monitor the temperature of the "water," but it also monitors indicators like acidity, oxygen content, and taste. A change in value on one of these indicators enables you to rapidly respond and to take pre-emptive action so that the quality of the "water" remains high. You create trust by sharing readings of this monitoring instrument to stakeholders. This trust will create a willingness to act and will contribute to realizing a successful change.

A change in value on an indicator can be positive as well as negative. You need to know either reading in order to steer the project towards its goal. The advantage of measuring multiple potential success indicators is that you can see potential project risks at an early stage in the project, so that you can deal with them before "damage is done." Monitoring potential success indicators is therefore a far more effective method of risk management than developing "what-if scenarios."

Capturing your project in a number of indicators has a very powerful psychological advantage. This advantage is that stakeholders tend to assess your project on the indicators that you give them. Other factors will, as it were, fade into the background. Psychologically, stakeholders will now be focused on the indicators for which they want to see an improvement. This wish to see an improvement makes it easier to prove an improvement.

## 6.6 Spin the Context

The potential success of your project can also be proved indirectly. This means that you influence the stakeholders' perception about potential success, by spinning the context. Spin doctors use this technique.

Basically, this technique entails to change the stakeholders' focus from the actual aim of the project to another issue associated with that aim. Whereas spin doctors often spin the context in order to conceal a problem, you can use it to let your proof of potential success relatively look better.

A classic example has become a government proposal to tax inheritance. Opponents called this a "death tax." By using this label, public opinion was diverted from taxing the rich to taxing the deceased. This change in the context has led to the situation that advocates of the tax had a hard time in convincing opponents of the "death tax."

To spin the context, you should not sell the desired change as a once-only change but as a continuous process of change of which your project is a part of.

You could also communicate the circumstances under which the solution is being developed (for example conflicts of interest, time pressure, unexpected obstacles). Explain how complex the starting situation was and what kind of setbacks you have encountered.

Elaborating on this context is very powerful in managing expectations, and as a consequence it becomes easier to meet these expectations. That is why a drawn game is celebrated as a victory after 10 losses. By showing how you overcame obstacles within the project, you will create trust in overcoming future obstacles. In other words, you then prove the potential success of your project.

Can the construction of the Sydney Opera House be regarded as a successful project? It has cost sixteen times more than estimated and took four times longer to build than planned.

Still, many people regard this project as successful. The Opera House is on the World Heritage list, has become a landmark for the city of Sydney, and attracts many visitors annually. Now we regard this project as a success, but if you consider the moment when the project was completed, one could see it as a failure.

# Benefits of SPOMP

A lthough each SPOMP strategy independently enhances the chance of a successful change project, it is above all the coherence between the strategies (Figure 19) that makes SPOMP a powerful approach.

You need to know which stakeholders to *seduce* (S) because otherwise it is not possible to plan the frequent communication moments (P) in your project. Knowing who to *seduce* is also imperative if you want to deploy the governance body to your advantage (O). Furthermore, frequent communication moments in your project enable multiple opportunities to market your change initiative (M) to stakeholders. Finally, to market your initiative, you need arguments, and these arguments are generated by proving the potential success of your project (P).

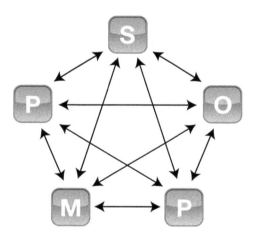

**Figure 19** Coherence between the SPOMP strategies

The SPOMP strategies combined significantly reduce resistance because stakeholders are taken along in the change process. It also dramatically increases support and buy-in because marketing and organizational politics are being utilized to positively influence the stakeholders' perception of the change.

The benefit of SPOMP is that you will become much more successful in *seducing* stakeholders into the change that you want to realize. Moreover, SPOMP holds many benefits for the client, the internal users, your project team members, the members of the governance body, and the organization as a whole.

### Benefits for the Client

The client often has to get accustomed to the process plan based on communication moments because of the early communication with stakeholders. The consequence of this early communication is that other stakeholders are allowed into the traditional black box which reduces the client's influence on the project.

The benefit for the client is, however, that he gets a solution, change strategy, and plan on how to implement organizational change he can do something with. There is no longer any doubt about adopting the recommendations or not. The client will adopt the recommendations because the internal consultant in charge has *seduced* stakeholders into the change. This means that there is already support in the organization, so the client no longer needs to hierarchically enforce the implementation of the recommended change.

### Benefits for the Internal Users

Internal users may feel overwhelmed by the SPOMP approach. From the moment that the process plan is presented, they are engaged in the project. As a consequence, they are made responsible for the outcome of the project. Internal users often experience a speeding up train that they have to get onto.

The benefit for internal users is, however, that they are not confronted with change. Internal users are invited to exchange their thoughts on how to implement change and their opinions are taken seriously. This influence gives them the opportunity to steer the project towards a solution that is applicable in their daily practice. It also provides internal users with the opportunity to synchronize the pace of the change dictated by the project with the everyday reality.

**Benefits for the Project Team Members**

At the start of the project, the members of the project team have to get accustomed to the shift in focus from the project management technique to *seducing* stakeholders into change.

The benefit for project team members is that the SPOMP approach is easy to follow because it has a logical structure. Project team members do not need to be trained in the specific peculiarities of a formal project management technique.[9]

Project team members are motivated to actively participate in the project because they designed the process plan in part themselves. They feel valued because their expertise is being used and listened to. SPOMP means for project team members to not only do the work but to be also responsible for a part of the project. They get the opportunity

---

[9] PMBOK, PRINCE2, MSP, RUP, Waterfall Method, Six Sigma, Business Process Redesign, Total Quality Management, Deming Cycle, IPMA, Dynamic Systems Development Method, EVO, OPEN, System Development Methodology, Scrum, ISO 21500, Agile, RUP, ... there are many project management techniques. Although they often have their origins in external consultancy, the advantage is that a common language and reference framework is created within the organization. This prevents terminology mix-ups and misunderstandings. The disadvantage is that the entire organization has to be trained in one project management technique in order to get maximum benefits.

to present the results of the subproject at a communication moment to various stakeholders. This opportunity makes them visible in the organization and fosters their career.

SPOMP finally has the benefit that careershapers are being engaged in the project. This makes it easier for project team members to show their diligence to their bosses. It also avoids any possible tension between the project team members' regular daily work and their loyalty to the project.

**Benefits for the Body Members**
Members of the governance body often have to get used to the fact that they are actually steering the project. The benefit of SPOMP for body members is that they are not only monitoring deviations from the project plan. In fact, their work in the body is getting significantly more interesting. This is because they now strategically can discuss with other body members about how to bridge different interests and how to achieve a successful change for the organization.

**Benefits for the Organization**
For the organization, the benefit of SPOMP is that the change will be realized successfully. In the beginning of the project, time needs to be invested because of the frequent communication moments. However, the total project duration will be significantly shorter because there is less resistance when implementing the change.

The benefit of SPOMP is also that the organizational or behavioral change becomes firmly anchored in the organization because there is much more commitment to the change. Furthermore, the learning and adaptive capability of the organization is strengthened by each successful SPOMPed project.

Finally, fewer resources are wasted on failed projects because with SPOMP potential resistance becomes visible at a much earlier stage in the project.

**Benefits for You**

For you, SPOMP means a fundamentally different way of project management. This is necessary because research shows that at present only one third of the projects are successful in realizing change (Appendix A). SPOMP can cause time pressure at the pre-planned communication moments, but from experience you will know how to handle that creatively. The benefit of SPOMP is that you will need less energy to lead your project team, because the goal of every communication moment is clear to project team members.

You will also need less energy to monitor and control the project because every project team member will feel responsible for meeting the deadlines that they have agreed upon themselves. As a consequence, you will evolve from a cop checking deadlines into a coach for your project team members. With SPOMP, you will manage successful projects, and so you will have a successful image within your organization. You will be noticed in your organization, and colleagues will be keen to cooperate with you. SPOMP ultimately has the benefit that it boosts your career within the organization. The next and final chapter of this book describes what to expect on your career path and how to increase your salary by 10 percent.

# And then…
# Making a Career

Your project is completed, and the intended organizational or behavioral change was successfully implemented in your organization. Before you take on the next project to SPOMP, you should take some time to think about your career.

As an internal professional, you have the intrinsic motivation to excel, but you also want to be valued in terms of respect from colleagues and adequately compensated as such. However, respect and a financial reward do not occur automatically. I-marketing is an absolute must to achieve this [5.4]. Therefore, you have to make sure that your accomplishments become visible to the right people [2.3.5] in your organization. The frequent communication moments in your project [3.0] provide an ideal platform for that.

You have to be consciously aware of the fact that your boss greatly benefits from your accomplishments. In fact, he delegated a part of his responsibilities disguised as a project to you. If you manage this project successfully, then your boss is also perceived as successful. That is why you should, right after your first successful SPOMPed projects, go up to your boss and ask him for a raise. As a coach, I often see that internal professionals quake at that, even when they are aware of their added value for the organization.

> Bach (2001) describes how you can increase your salary by 10 percent within nine weeks:[10]
>
> - Week 1: Stop complaining. Better to check out how many hours you are actually working for your boss. Telephone calls and internet

---

[10] Adapted from Bach, D., Smart couples finish rich, Broadway Books, New York, 2001, p. 247-272.

sessions outside working hours count, too. Compare your salary to that and calculate what you earn per hour worked.

- Week 2: Take a sheet of paper. Write on it your name, current salary, the raise that you want to ask for (for example 10 percent) and your salary plus the raise. Also, note today's date and the date in precisely two months' time. Because on that date you have to be ready to ask your boss for the raise. Hang this roadmap at home in a place where you will see it daily.[11]

- Week 3: Clear up all the clutter on your desk. Do this outside office hours because it is your mess. The piles of paper on your desk give others the impression that you are losing time and money. You will (subconsciously) be judged on that by your boss. With a clean desk you make a good impression: you are worth a raise. Then, you will even believe yourself that you are efficient. In short, make it visible to your boss that you are seriously striving to improve yourself.

- Week 4: Ask your boss for a five minute meeting. Take pen and paper with you. Explain that you are on a mission to improve the quality of your work for which you have read "HR Strategic Project Management SPOMP." Ask what your boss thinks of the work that you do already, what you could improve, and what value you could add for the organization. Write down his responses and tell him that you want to submit an action plan in a few days time. Type out the details and suggestions at home. Under that describe your action plan. Count on your boss being impressed by your initiative. Every boss wants a motivated employee like that.

- Week 5: Decide which part of your work is of most value to the organization and concentrate on that.

- Week 6: Find out what you can earn at other organizations. To do that, make some calls, look on the internet, and consult friends and colleagues.

---

[11] People who write down their targets supposedly have three times more chance of achieving that target.

- Week 7: Practice asking for a raise with a friend or partner, or out loud in front of a mirror. Explain at least six times, calmly and out loud, why you deserve the raise.

- Week 8: Ask for the raise. Better ask 10 percent extra than $10,000 annually because that sounds too dramatic. Chances are that your boss has become more aware of your capabilities, your contribution to the organization, and the amount of work that you take off his hands. This awareness helps you to get a raise and, in the worst case, in getting a bonus or in getting the opportunity to attend more courses, for example.

- Week 9: Reward yourself for your courage or for the result, even if you did not get anything extra.

Experience teaches us that internal professionals sometimes get stuck on the career ladder. Enormously appreciated, bonuses, but you keep on doing what you do. Your boss wants to retain you for his department because he cannot do without your efforts. Sometimes you are kept on a line, or given a lot of space. Everything will be done to keep you on, but you will not be making a career. Sometimes you are manipulated when it is suggested that in the future you can take the place of your boss. Even if that is the intention, you still will not be taking over his place. This is because the boss of your boss hardly knows you. Should this boss actually endorse your candidacy, then you probably will be eliminated in the selection process because other (higher) bosses in the organization do not know your reputation. That is why it is crucial for your career to include careershapers [2.3.5] in your projects.

How do you know that you are on the right path to a successful career? One of the signs that you are on the right path is jealous colleagues. You lead interesting projects and speak with many top executives, managers, and board members within the organization.

Another sign is that you are asked to manage ever more complex strategic projects. After that, there comes a phase where you can choose which projects you want to manage. The number of projects offered is larger than you can handle. Potential team members (colleagues) begin offering their services to participate in your next project. Management also asks you to let a "rookie" work along in your project. These are all signs that you are on the right path to making a successful career.

Now comes a decisive phase in your career. You need to choose between going into management or opting for a kind of coaching role as an internal professional. In both cases, your span of control is about 7 to 8 people. So, indirectly you will manage about 50 people in your organization when you are successful.

The choice is yours! "HR Strategic Project Management SPOMP" gives you the necessary strategies to become even more successful and to boost your career.

# Appendix A:
## Only 32 Percent of
## Projects are Successful

W hile doing research for this book, I was astonished by the success rate of projects. Various studies show that only 20-50 percent of the projects are successful.[12]

According to a study of IBM, most CEOs consider themselves and their organizations largely ineffective at implementing change.[13] This study cites a failure rate of almost 60 percent. The study also reveals that the percentage of CEOs who expect substantial change climbed from 65 percent in 2006 to 83 percent in 2008. However, CEOs reporting that they had successfully managed change in past rose just 4 percentage points, up from 57 percent in 2006 to 61 percent in 2008. The gap between the need for change and actual capability to deliver change has nearly tripled since the last study, in 2006.

One of the most comprehensive studies is done by The Standish Group. Since 1994, they have published every two years about the success and failure rates of projects. They use three categories to label a project:

- Succeeded: the project is completed on time, within budget, and of the agreed quality
- Challenged: the project is completed, but delivered later than planned and/or costs more than estimated and/or does not meet the initial requirements
- Failed: the project is cancelled before completion or is never implemented

---

[12] Studies like The Robbins-Gioia Survey (2001), The Conference Board Survey (2001), The KPMG Canada Survey (1997) and The OASIG Survey (1995), collectively identify a success rate of 20-50 percent, available at http://www.it-cortex.com/Stat_Failure_Rate.htm (last accessed February 11th 2012).

[13] IBM Corporation, Making change work, October 2008, available at http://www-935.ibm.com/services/us/gbs/bus/pdf/gbe03100-usen-03-making-change-work.pdf (last accessed November 3rd 2011).

The latest report shows that only 32 percent of more than 300,000 projects researched are successful.[14] A staggering 24 percent of the projects are a complete failure and 44 percent are challenged.

The percentage of successful projects has not much improved in the past 10 years. This is remarkable because in the past decade a lot of consultants and project managers have been trained in formal project management techniques such as PMBOK, PRINCE2, MSP, and Agile. However, research of The Standish Group shows that the formal project management technique only attributes 6 percent to the project's success.[15]

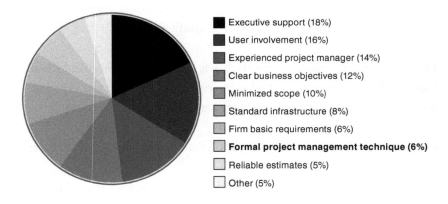

**Figure 20** Success factors in a project

---

[14] Press release from The Standish Group International Inc., April 23rd 2009, available at http://www.standishgroup.com/newsroom/chaos_2009.php (last accessed January 4th 2011).

[15] Johnson, J. et al., Collaborating on project success, The Standish Group International Inc., February/March 2001, available at http://www.softwaremag.com/archive/2001feb/collaborativemgt.html (last accessed October 4th 2010).

The two most important success factors (Figure 20) are creating support from executives (the client) and involving users (the internal user) in your project. The five strategies presented in this book show you how you can *seduce* both to support and buy into the change you want to realize with your project. Applying these strategies will significantly reduce resistance to the change and make you much more successful as an internal consultant, project manager, program manager, management consultant, change agent, or change manager.

# Appendix B:
Nobody Actually Likes
Change

An organizational change requires per definition from various people within the organization a change in behavior, attitude, or working method. For example, a project to introduce new payroll software leads to a new way of working. A project aimed to simplify a certain form leads to people having to learn how to fill out the new form in a different way than they are used to. An implementation of a new recruitment and selection strategy leads to various people having to adjust the way they currently work. The more strategic the project, the more fundamental and invasive the behavioral change is that you have to realize.

A behavioral change is challenging to realize because people in general do not actually like to change their behavior. This is because most people do not like to exchange a safe and familiar way of working for an unknown one. Even if you show them the imperfections of the current situation and the benefits of the new situation, the majority of people will still be reluctant to change.

The "imbalance in benefits" makes realizing a behavioral change also challenging. A solution for a problem is often that one group has to do something so that another group can benefit. For example, if executives believe that the throughput of talent is too low, then line managers have to make an extra effort to identify talents in their department. You will have the support and commitment from executives because they will get an advantage out of the project. The question, however, is how do you motivate line managers to seriously scout for additional talent? Which advantages will line managers get out of your project?

The solution to these challenges is to make the behavioral change desirable for every individual stakeholder. In other words, you will have to create a demand for the change that you want to realize. You can create a demand by selling your change initiative to stakeholders and by positively influencing them to support your project [5.0]. By doing so, you will make the minds of the stakeholders receptive to your ideas, and this greatly enhances your chances to realize a successful behavioral change.

# Acknowledgements

Writing a book is comparable to managing a change project. Both are intellectual challenges where you can only succeed by working together. In both cases, you choose who you need in order to achieve the best possible result and to whom you communicate at the agreed communication moments.

Therefore, I first identified a number of successful project managers, change agents, academics, and other critical professionals and divided them into two target groups. I wanted to present to the first target group the concept of my book in order to let them look into my black box. The communication moment with this group was almost two years ago. Aaron Hobbs, MBA, Angelique Rousseau, BA, Alex Barlas, PhD, Matthea Connelley, BA, and Wesley Matthews, PhD, thank you very much for your constructive comments and your help in improving my book.

The second target group was willing to review the final draft of my book: Andre and Neeke Collins, Annemieke Wozniak, BA, Astrid Fox, BA, Auke and Saakje Maxwell, Corrien Columbus, PhD, Elise Vey, BA, Fred Durham, BA, Harold Rodriguez, BA, Henrike Maschke, LLM, Jonathan Cartwright, Jornt Letourneau, BA, Dr. Marc Steinmetz, Marc Peabody, BA, Maryvonne Webb, LLM, Matt Hu, PhD, Raja Mukhtar, PhD, Renaud Robertson, MBA, Roos Villarreal, BA, Dr. Siedo Nazario, Sip and Marian Torres, Stan Szymanski, MBA, Tony Wu, BA, and all others who contributed, many thanks for fine-tuning my ideas, honing my mind and your moral support.

I also owe my thanks to Annie Breeuwsma, Darline Spring, Fester Koekoek, Leslie Feldman, Stephen Cook, and Taeko Beerda. Leslie and Stephen are my language providers. They ensured that my message is worded properly. Darline masterfully edited the manuscript by injecting her experience as a registered Project Management Professional (PMP). Annie and Fester are from "packaging." They creatively designed this book to make it visually attractive. Taeko is responsible for the online support. He developed the easily navigable websites www.leonhielkema.com and www.seducestakeholders.com. Heartfelt thanks to you all for your input and assistance.

In particular I would like to thank Ankie Swakhoven, BA/MBA. Ankie has been my intellectual sounding board in writing this book from the start. She has brought structure to my ideas about project and change management, and supplied many ideas to improve my book even further. Ankie, I owe you a lot of gratitude, and I hope that you are willing to collaborate with me in writing my subsequent books.

I would like to close out the acknowledgements by thanking Mirjam Boelens, PhD. Mirjam gave me the opportunity to write this book. She assessed concepts, relentlessly challenged my ideas, and among many other things, inspired me to push my limits. Thank you very, very much Mirjam for all your help.

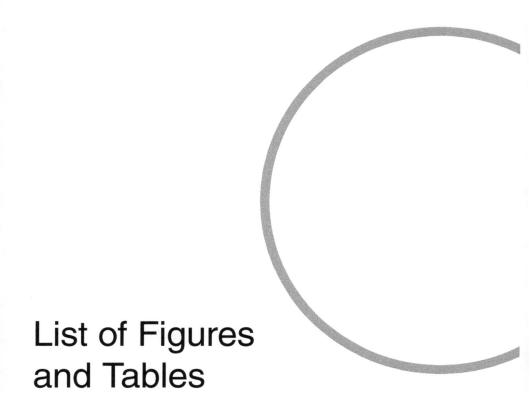

# List of Figures
# and Tables

# Index

U-turn, 77–79

V
Variety of interests, 88
Virtual teams, 5
Visibility, 76, 108, 140, 145
Visualize data, 110

W
Well-balanced soccer team, 44
What-if scenarios, 131
When to seduce, 59–81
Who to seduce, 35–56
Willingness to act, 116, 122, 127
Work products
*See* Communication message
Works Council, 48

# Links

Please visit www.SeduceStakeholders.com/links for updated links where you can leave your comments on Amazon, Barnes & Noble, Goodreads, iBooks, and many more. Your comments will help others in judging whether this book is suited to their specific situations. Thank you in advance!

This page also contains trusted links to my blog and social media venues like Facebook, Google+, LinkedIn, and Twitter. I am looking forward to hear from you!

# HR Strategic Project Management PLUS

The most crucial phase of every change project is the project initiation phase. In this phase, you will actually lay down the foundation for a successful project. About 80 percent of this foundation will be constructed in collaboration with your client. "HR Strategic Project Management PLUS" (expected 2013/2014) will give you new powerful insights on how to:

- Create a strong negotiating position toward the client
- Distill the actual project goal concealed in the initial project assignment
- Align the project with the organization's strategic mission

The remaining part of the foundation will be constructed in collaboration with your project team. The aim is to efficiently develop a process plan and present it to the client and other stakeholders. "HR Strategic Project Management PLUS" will give you new powerful insights on how to:

- Jump-start your project by strategically preparing the first meeting with your project team
- Forge individual project team members into a winning collective
- Inspire project team members to follow your lead

By applying the insights of "HR Strategic Project Management PLUS" in the project initiation phase, you will exceed the expectations of the client, your project team members, and other stakeholders. You will create a strong foundation that enables you to steer your project towards success.

Go to www.SeduceStakeholders.com/win now for details on a monthly chance to obtain "HR Strategic Project Management PLUS" for **free!**

Your name in "HR Strategic Project Management PLUS"?

Do you have practical examples or interesting insights that complement the SPOMP strategies and/or the project initiation phase that you would like to share? Please email me your contribution to *plus@leonhielkema.com*. The most interesting contributions will be included in my next book "HR Strategic Project Management PLUS," with your name credited as contributor. Your contribution gives the reader even more interesting insights on how to realize a successful change, and it provides you personally invaluable I-marketing!